The Startup Self-Check

Build a Business That Won't Inherit Your Baggage

By Brent Whistler

Startup Self Check

Copyright © 2025 Brent Whistler

https://www.buildrunkit.com

All rights reserved. No part of this publication may be reproduced, distributed, or transmitted in any form or by any means — electronic or mechanical — including photocopying, recording, or by any information storage and retrieval system, without the prior written permission of the publisher, except in the case of brief quotations embodied in critical reviews and certain other noncommercial uses permitted by copyright law.

For bulk orders, educational licenses, permission requests or speaking inquiries, visit:
https://brkit.vip/sf-business

Library of Congress Control Number: 2026902710

ISBN: 979-8-9931758-0-5

First Edition, 2026

Published by BuildRunKit Media, Lago Vista, TX United States

https://www.buildrunkit.com

Printed in the United States of America

This book is a work of nonfiction. Some names and identifying details may have been changed to protect the privacy of individuals.

To my mom, because she supports everything that I do and she tells me when I'm being a dimwit in the gentlest way possible.

To my husband for being by my side, all the while letting me stay in my office couped up A LOT!

And to all the frustrated, bright-faced founders who feel like they don't have support and direction they need to get a business started. I hope you'll let me be a nutritious part of your journey!

Acknowledgments
Thanks to Tisaz Studio for the killer cover design,
Bernadette Ferreira for editing help and content organization

Contents

Why Purpose Comes First 1

Rewiring Identity 13

Strengths, Skills & Blind Spots 23

Beliefs About Money 32

Designing Your Life 43

Habits & Focus 57

Support Systems 74

Burnout Prevention 89

Personal Runway 104

Putting It All Together 123

Bonus Chapter: Your Personal Brand 133

|  | I know this isn't usually allowed, but SKIP TO THE END for a minute! Down there, you can take a second to check out the resources available to you on our website and download and print the companion document to this book, so you will be able to take notes if you want. |

Ok – now..

Why Purpose Comes First

Introduction: Why This Chapter Matters

Let's be clear about something upfront: purpose isn't optional.

It's not a slogan you slap on a slide deck and forget about. It's the bedrock. The compass. The thing everything else sits on. If you're trying to build a startup without a clear reason for why you're doing it, you're building on sand.

A lot of founders jump into business because they see an opportunity - a trend, a clever product idea, a gap that looks profitable. That's fine. That can get you moving. But it won't carry you very far.

Because when things get difficult - and they will - opportunity alone isn't enough. Without a clear sense of purpose, you start second-guessing every decision. You lose momentum. You drift. And eventually, you burn out or walk away.

I've seen it happen more times than I can count.

This chapter matters because misalignment between your business and your values is one of the top reasons people burn out or abandon their ventures. I've seen talented, ambitious entrepreneurs build something "successful" by external standards - only to realize they hate the day-to-day of running it. That's a tragedy you can avoid.

> **Brent's Thoughts™** See, I didn't always know this stuff. When I first decided to quit Microsoft and start my own business, I decided to create a business that solved my problem (I hate doing laundry). So, I started a wash-and-fold business called Drive-By Laundry. Guess who ended up doing the two things he hated: driving and doing laundry? I was so excited with the mechanics of starting a business, and I wanted to learn and learn and learn, but that curiosity wasn't going to sustain me long-term. There's only so much to learn in the laundry business.

When your business aligns with your deeper motivations, you're not chasing profit; you're building something that feels meaningful. That's life-aligned entrepreneurship. You get to grow your company *and* live a life you're proud of.

So, before you start sketching out product features or setting revenue targets, we're going to take a step back. This is your chance to connect your personal values with your business vision. That connection will guide everything that comes next - your brand, your decisions, your marketing, your team, your offers.

You'll leave this chapter with more than just warm fuzzies. You'll leave with a framework to define your purpose, vet your ideas, and make decisions faster. Because when you know why you're here, the "how" gets a whole lot easier.

Let's dig in.

What 'Purpose' Really Means in Business

> Purpose isn't just what you do. It's why you do it, and that "why" becomes the emotional engine of your business.

Let's be real: there will be weeks when the money isn't flowing, customers are ghosting, and you're questioning your life choices. On those days, you need more than a sales target to keep you going. You need emotional fuel. That's what purpose gives you. Imagine if you're starving and poor, but your job is still to hand out sweet puppies to nice old ladies (on a temporary basis, because otherwise, you're just making that sweet grandma work). At least you're doing something that brings you joy! On the other hand - imagine that you're driving around in the snow, cursing traffic, delivering laundry orders to ingrates.

Think about the founders behind brands like Patagonia, Spanx, or Basecamp. They didn't just start companies - they started movements.

Patagonia's purpose is to protect the planet, and it guides every product and marketing decision they make.

Spanx didn't begin as a shapewear company; it began as Sara Blakely's mission to help women feel confident.

Basecamp wasn't just about project management; it was about creating a calmer, saner way to work.

When you know your purpose, you can make decisions faster and more confidently. You stop chasing shiny objects and focus on what aligns with your deeper mission. You know which opportunities to say yes to - and which ones to walk away from, even if they're profitable.

If ever you wonder, "why is that guy running a business that's never going to make him rich," you've just discovered a truth: we're not robots! Logic doesn't drive all the decision making. We must make room for what motivates us and makes us feel like we're doing the thing we were meant to do.

> **Brent's Thoughts™** I might not get rich doing what I do now, but I'm teaching people to do what I sorely needed help to learn when I was starting my first businesses, and I'm coding helpful tools! These are things I'm passionate about, and if you see me out and about at conferences, you might guess that I love to travel too, and you'd be right!
>
> What is it in your work life or personal life that you just love to do - not just the outcomes but the actual activities? Maybe start your thought process there.

Here's what makes it easy: your purpose doesn't have to be world changing. It doesn't have to end climate change or feed a million kids. But it does need to matter to you. If you care deeply about giving freelancers more freedom, or helping single parents save time, or making software that's fun instead of frustrating - that's enough. Purpose is personal.

When you infuse your business with that kind of personal meaning, customers feel it. Employees rally around it. And you? You'll be a hell of a lot more likely to stick with it through the inevitable ups and downs.

The Purpose Pyramid

The Purpose Pyramid

Let's break it down. If purpose feels a little abstract, I've got a model to help: the Purpose Pyramid. It's a simple, three-layer framework that brings clarity and focus to your business.

Layer 1: Why I Care

At the base is your emotional core. This is personal. It's the story behind the story - why this business matters to you. Maybe you struggled with something and now want to help others avoid the same pain. Maybe you had a transformative experience and want to spread that magic. Maybe you're just obsessed with making things better, smarter, or more beautiful. This is your reason for showing up.

Layer 2: Who I Serve

Next, get specific about your audience. Who benefits from this business? Not a demographic - real people. Picture them. What do they struggle with? What do they aspire to? A clear purpose always includes a clear who. Without that, you're just broadcasting into the void.

Layer 3: What I'll Create

Finally, the output. What are you building? A tool? A service? A movement? A platform? This is where you start to get concrete, but it comes last for a reason. If you define the "what" before the "why" and "who," you risk building something nobody needs - or worse, something you don't even like.

Let's apply it:

Why I care: I hated how hard it was to learn bookkeeping as a solopreneur.
Who I serve: Freelancers who want to feel in control of their finances.
What I'll create: A friendly, no-jargon budgeting app that teaches while it tracks.

You've got clarity, and you're focused.

Once you fill out your own Purpose Pyramid, you've got a north star. You've gone from building a thing to building a thing on purpose.

How to Find Your Purpose (If You're Not Sure Yet)

Not everyone wakes up one morning with a lightning bolt of purpose. If you're sitting there thinking, "I don't know my purpose," don't panic. You're not broken - you just haven't asked the right questions yet.

Start by looking inward. Here are some prompts that have helped the business coaches in my life discover what makes their aspiring founders tick:

- What problems have I faced that I'm now uniquely positioned to help solve?
- What topics or issues do I find myself ranting about (in a good way)?
- When I picture a "perfect" day of work, what am I doing - and who am I helping?
- If I could make one part of the world suck less, what would it be?

You might also look backward. What moments in your life shaped your worldview? What injustices, annoyances, or gaps made you say, "Someone should really fix this"? Sometimes your purpose was hiding in plain sight all along.

And if nothing comes up immediately? Try prototyping. Seriously. Go help someone with something you care about. Start a project. Write a blog. Teach a mini course. Action creates clarity. As you move, you'll start to notice which problems you care about solving - and which ones drain you.

One important note: don't get stuck trying to find your forever purpose. Purpose evolves. You're not getting married to this version of your "why" - you're just committing to what feels meaningful right now. Give yourself permission to evolve.

Clarity will come, not from navel-gazing forever, but from taking purpose-aligned action again and again.

> **Brent's Thoughts™** Purpose comes in many forms, and it doesn't have to be fancy. It can even be selfish!
>
> You know one of my biggest drivers? I need to keep my mind constantly busy. If I don't wear myself out, the internal chaos just doesn't stop.
>
> That's where the BuildRunKit came from: an endless pipeline of tools, frameworks, and value-adds I can keep building for others.
>
> So now, I never have to ask, "Is there anything to do?"
>
> There are always a thousand tiny tasks that keep the dopamine flowing.

Using Purpose as a Filter for Ideas & Goals

Purpose isn't just for branding - it's your best filter for strategy.

When you're drowning in ideas or trying to figure out which project deserves your time and energy, purpose helps you prioritize. Ask yourself: *Does this move me closer to my deeper mission?* If not, let it go.

Let's say you're a founder whose purpose is to help small business owners feel less overwhelmed. You get an opportunity to partner with a fintech company that's big on automation - but their brand tone is aggressive and hustle-heavy. Does it align? Probably not. Walk away.

Or let's say you're trying to decide between building a course, launching a podcast, or writing a book. Instead of chasing what's trendy, use your purpose to pick what best serves your audience and fuels your energy. When your choices align with your purpose, you're more likely to finish them - and more likely to attract the right audience.

This isn't just about saying "no" to things that are off-track. It's also about saying "hell yes" to things that align, even if they scare you. If something feels purpose-aligned but daunting, that's usually a green light. The resistance is just your brain protecting you from risk - not telling you it's wrong.

Here's a litmus test I give to friends to use when I'm in the advice-giving mood:

> **Will this make my future self proud?**

If the answer is yes, you're probably on the right track.

Founders waste months - sometimes years - on business detours that felt exciting in the moment but had nothing to do with their core purpose. You can't afford that. Use purpose like a compass, and your journey gets a whole lot straighter.

Wrap-Up + What's Next

Let's recap.
Purpose is not optional. It's not something you sprinkle on top of your branding like cilantro on tacos. It's the root of sustainable entrepreneurship. Without it, your business becomes a grind. With it, your business becomes a reflection of who you are and what you care about.

In this chapter, we defined what purpose really means - it's your emotional fuel, your decision filter, your leadership engine. We broke it down into the

Purpose Pyramid: why you care, who you serve, and what you'll create. We talked about how to uncover your purpose if it isn't clear yet. And we showed how purpose makes decision-making easier, faster, and more aligned.

In short: purpose isn't soft. It's strategic. It helps you build something that *lasts* - and feels worth it.

Next up, we're going to build on this foundation by diving into your identity as a founder - not just who you are now, but who you're becoming. We'll explore the beliefs, values, and behaviors that shape the way you lead, build, and show up in your business.

When you combine Purpose with Personal Clarity, you stop trying to fit into someone else's mold - and start building a business that fits you.

See you in Chapter 2.

Rewiring Identity

Founder Discovered

Stepping Out of the Shadow

One of the most overlooked transformations in entrepreneurship isn't in your business model, it's in your identity. The shift from employee to founder isn't just logistical. It's psychological, and in many ways it's deeply personal. It's even raw, because you're exposing yourself to the world, and you finally have to admit that you can't hide behind "they" anymore ("They don't let us do that.." .. "They said I have to increase sales by 20%.."). It's all you. You're about to really learn about accountability - to the person it's hardest to be accountable to: yourself.

Early in the founder journey, you might find yourself operating in the shadows of old patterns. You second-guess your instincts. You wait for permission. You hesitate to claim your space. Even though you've technically started your own thing, your identity hasn't quite caught up. You're a founder on paper, but in practice, you're still behaving like a well-trained employee. That's normal.

I call this phase stepping out of the shadow. It's the awkward in-between where you're no longer fully aligned with your past role but haven't yet grown into the awesome and scary pile of autonomous self-determination of your new role. And it's sneaky, because the shadow might not just be from a previous boss or company. Sometimes it's the shadow of your own inner critic. Or your parents' expectations. Or a peer group that doesn't understand your ambition.

This is why identity work is so critical. Without rewiring how you see yourself, you'll unconsciously recreate the same systems and barriers you were trying to escape from and overcome. You'll underprice, overwork, avoid risk, apologize for your ambition.

Founders who succeed in the long run aren't smarter or luckier. They own the founder identity-even when it feels scary. Even before they feel "ready." That confidence? It's not bravado. It's a result of doing the inner work to fully step into the role they've chosen.

And that's what this chapter is about: rewiring your internal operating system to match the role you're building externally. This is where things start to shift for good.

> **Brent's Thoughts™** Try to be super-aware of imposter syndrome seeping into your psyche. That jerk has to be faced head on. For years, when people would find out that I had programmed at Microsoft, I would follow up with something like, "Yeah, but I wasn't the caliber of programmer Microsoft would hire. I came through an acquisition." In fact, I still hear garbage like that come out of my mouth sometimes. You know what, though? As much as I didn't feel like a "real" programmer compared to colleagues, I wrote just as much code as they did, and I was acquired for business domain expertise anyway! Did any of those fancy programmers know about financial reporting? Not like I did! I was a real boy the whole time! And you? You're really doing it. That thing, what you're doing now.. that's called doing it.

The Identity Shift Diagram

IDENTITY SHIFT DIAGRAM

Old Identity	The Shift	New Identity
• Core beliefs: "I'm not ready" / "I'm not that kind of person" • Habits: Avoids visibility, overprepares, overthinks • Emotional state: Hesitant, protective	• Moment of tension, challenge, or commitment • Key reframe: "What if I already am?" • New choice: act despite discomfort	• Core beliefs: "I do hard things," "This is who I am now" • Habits: Shows up visibly, sets boundaries, experiments publicly • Emotional state: Uncomfortable but grounded

Let's visualize what's happening when you move from employee to entrepreneur. I call it the *Identity Shift Diagram*-and it's a simple three-stage arc:

Current Identity → Transition Phase → Entrepreneurial Identity

Stage 1: Current Identity

This is where most of us start. You've been trained to operate as a cog in a larger system. You follow structure. You optimize for performance reviews. You're rewarded for compliance, not risk. In this stage, safety and stability are top priorities-and that's not bad. But it is limiting if you want to build something your way.

Stage 2: Transition Phase

This is the messy middle. You've left the structure behind, but haven't fully embodied your new role yet. It feels shaky. Uncertain. You might flip-flop between "This is the best decision of my life" and "What the hell am I doing?"- sometimes in the same hour. Welcome to the identity gym.

This phase is critical. It's where the real rewiring begins. You're shedding the thought patterns that no longer serve you, while building the muscle of entrepreneurial thinking.

Common signs you're in this stage:

- You feel guilty setting your own rates.
- You hesitate to market yourself.
- You look for external validation before taking action.
- You're overly busy but not getting traction.

That's not failure. That's friction, and friction means transformation is underway.

Stage 3: Entrepreneurial Identity

This is where things click. You stop waiting for permission. You start seeing yourself as the leader of your own mission. You take ownership of your time, your energy, your vision. Your decisions feel bolder-but also cleaner.

This doesn't mean you've figured everything out. But it does mean you're building from your own center. And that changes everything.

When you understand the Identity Shift Diagram, you can stop beating yourself up for not "being further along." You're not behind, you're in process. And that's exactly where you need to be.

> **Brent's Thoughts℠** Hey - you know when I knew I had made the shift? It's when I started making the rules, sticking to the rules and intentionally pissing off my worst customers so they'd self-select out. Pro tip: The customers who always want you to break the rules are the same ones that will nickel and dime you into the grave and make you wish you hadn't come to work - but that's for another chapter. Actually, that's a couple of books down the road.

From Employee to Entrepreneur

Let's get practical. What does it look like to rewire your mindset from employee to founder?

Start with this: an employee trades time for predictability. A founder trades certainty for possibility.

That one shift touches everything, from how you price your work to how you deal with setbacks. But it doesn't happen overnight. It takes practice. Let's walk through some of the most important mental rewires:

Employee Mindset	Entrepreneur Mindset
"Tell me what to do."	"What problem am I solving and how?"
"I hope they pick me."	"I'm building something worth choosing."
"I get paid for hours worked."	"I get paid for value delivered."
"Mistakes are bad; stay safe."	"Mistakes are data; learn fast."
"Don't rock the boat."	"Take up space and lead boldly."

If you've spent years-or decades-operating in employee mode, these shifts will feel weird at first. You might feel uncomfortable charging more, promoting yourself, or saying no. That's okay. That's part of the rewiring.

Now you're building capacity. Emotional, financial, creative. And that means stepping into discomfort repeatedly until it becomes your new normal.

One powerful exercise: start noticing the language you use. Do you say, "my little side hustle" or "my business"? Do you say, "I'm trying" or "I'm building"? Language shapes identity. Identity shapes results.

> **Brent's Thoughts™** Just now, after decades, I'm finally settling into more powerful language and a more realistic vocabulary when it comes to my business and my worth.

Remember: being an entrepreneur isn't about having a certain personality. It's about making decisions in alignment with your future self. You don't become that person before you act. You become that person by acting.

Embodying the Founder Role

You don't become a founder just by filing an LLC or launching a landing page. You embody the founder role through daily actions that reinforce your new identity.

This part is subtle but powerful. It's about creating micro-signals that tell your brain, "This is who I am now."

Let's break it down:

Language

Start with how you introduce yourself. Say "I run a company" even if you're the only employee. Own your title. Replace "just" and "trying" with clear, declarative language. This rewires your internal narrative in real time.

Boundaries

Founders protect their time. That means blocking work hours-even if no one's asking for your time yet. It means saying no to energy-draining obligations, even if they're familiar. Employees often wait until they're "busy" to set boundaries. Entrepreneurs set boundaries to create the space to grow.

Rituals

Create routines that support your role. CEOs don't just roll out of bed and check Slack. They set priorities, review metrics, reflect on vision. Even if your version is a morning journal and 30 minutes of focused work, the intention matters.

> **Brent's Thoughts™** I'm probably not the best person to be talking about founder / executive rituals. Oops - see - there I go again with that self-defeating language. Let's say it like this: My ritual is very simple. I use early morning to swap between feeding my need for scandal and gossip (YouTube, Facebook) to researching and solving problems to falling back to sleep for a few minutes. My deepest brainstorms and planning exercises happen between 5am and 7am before I've even gotten out of bed.

Environment

Surround yourself with things and people that reflect who you're becoming. That could mean working in a clean, inspiring space or joining a founder community that challenges you to level up. Identity is contagious.

This is how transformation happens: not in a single epiphany, but in dozens of tiny decisions that reinforce your new role.

Every time you act from your founder identity, you strengthen it. And eventually, it's not something you're "trying on." It's just who you are.

Wrap-Up + What's Next

This chapter wasn't about tactics-it was about transformation. Before you master your pitch, your funnel, or your pricing model, you've got to master your internal operating system.

Here's what we covered:

- The shift from employee to entrepreneur isn't automatic. It requires identity rewiring.
- You may start your business still living in the shadow of old roles, habits and stories.
- The Identity Shift Diagram helps you locate where you are and normalize the transition phase.
- We outlined key mindset shifts and the daily practices that help you embody the founder role, not just imagine it.

If Chapter 1 was about aligning your *purpose*, this chapter was about aligning yourself. And those two together create unstoppable clarity.

In Chapter 3, we'll turn inward again. This time, we're going to inventory your strengths, surface the skills that set you apart, and shine a light on the blind spots that might be holding you back. Because building a great business doesn't start with what the world wants. It starts with knowing exactly what you bring to the table.

See you there.

Strengths, Skills & Blind Spots

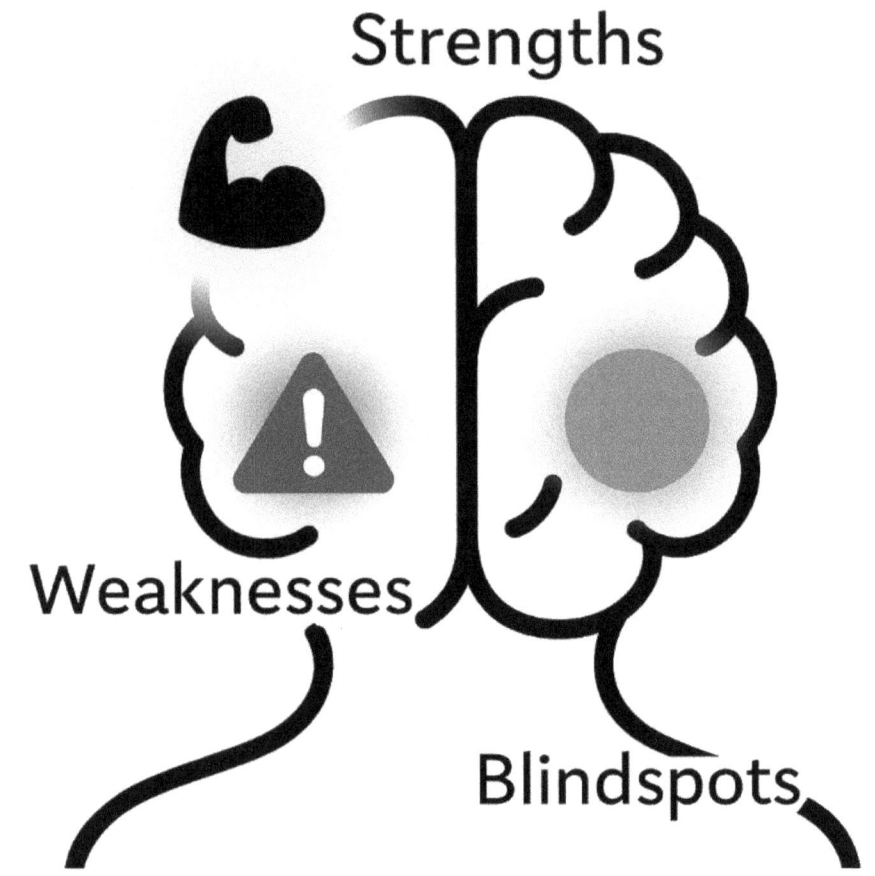

Knowing Your Toolbelt

Let's start with a hard truth: many first-time founders drastically underestimate how much they already bring to the table.

You've probably been taught to value credentials, job titles, or hard skills you can list on a resume. But entrepreneurship doesn't care what your LinkedIn says. It cares whether you can solve problems, adapt fast and keep moving when everything's on fire. And for that, you need to know your toolbelt.

> **Brent's Thoughts™** If you're someone like me who has no formal education beyond high school, this is even more critical! Your toolbox is your calling card. Don't be meek! You've got to lead with your knowledge and to do that, you have to take inventory and know where you excel. Oh, and spend all your extra time learning. I ain't got no college degree, but there is knowledge oozing out of my brain onto the floor, because I never stop learning!

Think of your strengths and skills like a well-worn set of tools. Some are obvious: copywriting, sales, coding, operations. Others are quiet but powerful: pattern recognition, emotional intelligence, grit, diplomacy. The problem is, if you don't take inventory early on, you'll default to using the same 2-3 tools you're most comfortable with-and ignore the rest.

And here's where things get dicey: if your default tools don't match the needs of your stage of business, you create drag. Let's say you're an incredible product builder-but allergic to marketing. If you ignore that gap, your brilliant product might stay invisible. On the flip side, if you're a natural community builder but always force yourself to do solo execution, you'll burn out in silence.

> **Brent's Thoughts™** Hey! Guess why Drive-By Laundry never netted me more than a few hundred dollars per month? Because I am a terrible marketer! Now I let other people do that!

Strengths, Skills & Blind Spots

That's why this chapter exists. We're not here to slap labels on you-we're here to increase your awareness. Because when you know what's in your toolbelt, you get to make strategic choices: what to lean into, what to outsource, what to avoid entirely.

You are not supposed to be great at everything. No founder is. But the founders who win? They know what they're great at and they build around it, not against it.

The Founder SWOT Analysis

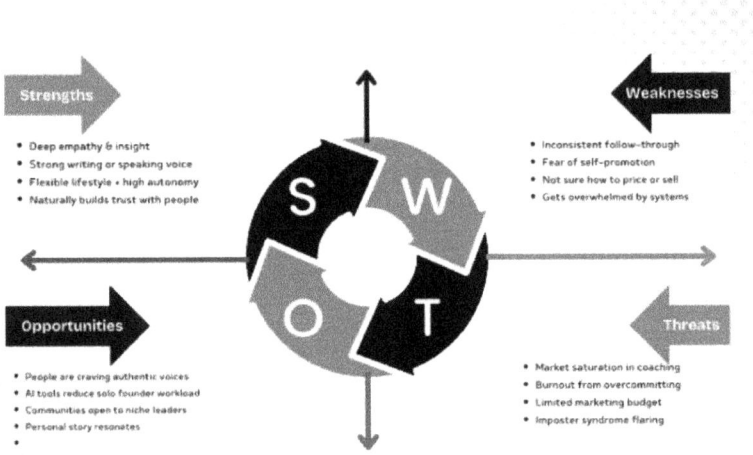

You've probably seen a SWOT analysis before - Strengths, Weaknesses, Opportunities, Threats. Most of the time it's stuck in a static 2x2 grid on some dusty business school slide. I mean, I'm guessing? I didn't go to business school.

And yeah, that grid is fine. But startups aren't tidy. They aren't static. And they definitely are not theoretical.

So, let's bring SWOT down to earth.

Enter the Founder's SWOT - a grounded, founder-focused version that connects your internal reality (strengths + weaknesses) with the external forces shaping your path (opportunities + threats).

This isn't just a planning tool. It's a clarity check. Something of a snapshot of where you stand before you try to build something big.

Let's break it down:

Strengths

These are your superpowers; the things that come easily, feel energizing, and get results. They're not always obvious. Sometimes we undervalue our strengths because they feel too easy. (Hint: If people often say, "you're so good at that!" and you shrug it off, it's probably a strength.)

Strengths can be skills (like persuasive writing), traits (like resilience), or learned habits (like deep focus). Startups thrive when founders build around these.

Weaknesses / Blind Spots

This isn't about shame-it's about visibility. Weaknesses are things you don't do well, and things you consistently avoid. Blind spots, however, are the ones you don't realize are dragging you down.

A few common ones: perfectionism, conflict avoidance, procrastinating big-picture strategy in favor of busy work. The danger isn't in having weaknesses. It's in pretending they don't exist.

Opportunities

Here's where strengths meet timing. What external trends, gaps, or needs align with what you're uniquely equipped to offer? This is where traction often lives. Maybe you're a killer at video content, and there's an underserved niche in your industry hungry for that format. That's opportunity, and it's yours to claim.

Threats

These aren't just about competition. They include mindset traps, misalignment, and any recurring patterns that could undermine your growth. For instance, if you over-commit to clients because you hate saying no, that's a threat to your capacity. If your business depends on one fragile platform (hello, Instagram algorithm), that's a threat to stability.

Your SWOT diagram gives you clarity. When you understand the pieces and plan around them, you accelerate. You know exactly where to adjust. This isn't a one-time exercise. It's a living check-in.

So, let's assess.

Founder Mini-Assessment

Think of this as your personal calibration. The point isn't to be "right," but rather to reflect honestly. Grab a notebook or open a doc, and spend a few minutes with these questions:

Mini-Assessment: Strengths & Skills

What do people consistently come to me for help with?

What tasks feel easy for me but hard for others?

When do I feel most in flow or "on fire" creatively?

What do I *enjoy* doing-even when I'm tired?

What am I proud of creating, solving, or leading in the past?

Mini-Assessment: Blind spots & Drains

What types of work do I put off, even if I'm technically capable?

What situations trigger anxiety, frustration, or imposter syndrome?

What feedback have I received more than once that I resisted?

What skills am I tired of using (even if I'm good at them)?

When have I taken on too much or played too small?

Now, synthesize:

- Write down your **Top 5 Strengths**
  (Use actual words like "systems thinking" or "empathetic communication.")

- Write down **3 Blind spots or Challenges**
  (These are invitations-not criticisms.)

This is your personal founder fingerprint. No one else has the exact combo you do. And knowing it? That's power.

Because now, instead of flailing through trial and error, you've got a lens. You know what you bring into every room-and what to watch for when stress hits.

We're not doing a full SWOT here - not yet. Opportunities and Threats will come later, once we've explored your market and audience.

First, we need to get grounded in you - the internal half.

That means surfacing your Strengths and Weaknesses (or as I like to call them, Blind Spots & Drains). This isn't a resume. It's a radar check.

That said, feel free to start noticing where you might develop opportunities to mitigate weaknesses or lean into strengths.

And if you want to dip a toe into threats, try this:

What personal patterns might put your momentum or your project at risk?

Putting It All Together

You now have something most founders don't: self-awareness in motion.

This chapter wasn't about building skills from scratch-it was about surfacing what's already there, often just below the surface. That awareness becomes your advantage. It lets you design roles, processes, and even offers that play to your edge.

Here's the rule I give to my mentees:

> **Build your business to amplify your strengths, not just fill your calendar.**

Let's say your strengths are storytelling, teaching, and energizing people. You might double down on content-led marketing, create a founder-led podcast, or teach high-ticket workshops. But if your daily schedule is filled with admin, tech troubleshooting, and solo implementation? You're building the wrong business around the right person.

> **Brent's Thoughts℠** My friend Tina was a professional organizer for years. She's annoyingly tidy and just neat as a pin (can't stand her! Kidding!). If I had gone into that business, it would clearly be because my dog ate my SWOT. I can't be depended on to put the toilet lid down or make the bed, let alone organize things for a living!

This chapter is your permission slip to design around your natural energy. Use the SWOT diagram quarterly. Revisit your toolbelt often. Your skills and context will change, but your job as founder is to keep aligning.

Next up: money.
Not just what you charge, but what you believe.

Chapter 4 is about your financial wiring: how your past, your culture, and your inner critic shape how you think about earning and asking.

If you don't face your beliefs about money, they *will* shape your business, whether you like it or not.

Let's go find out how.

Beliefs About Money

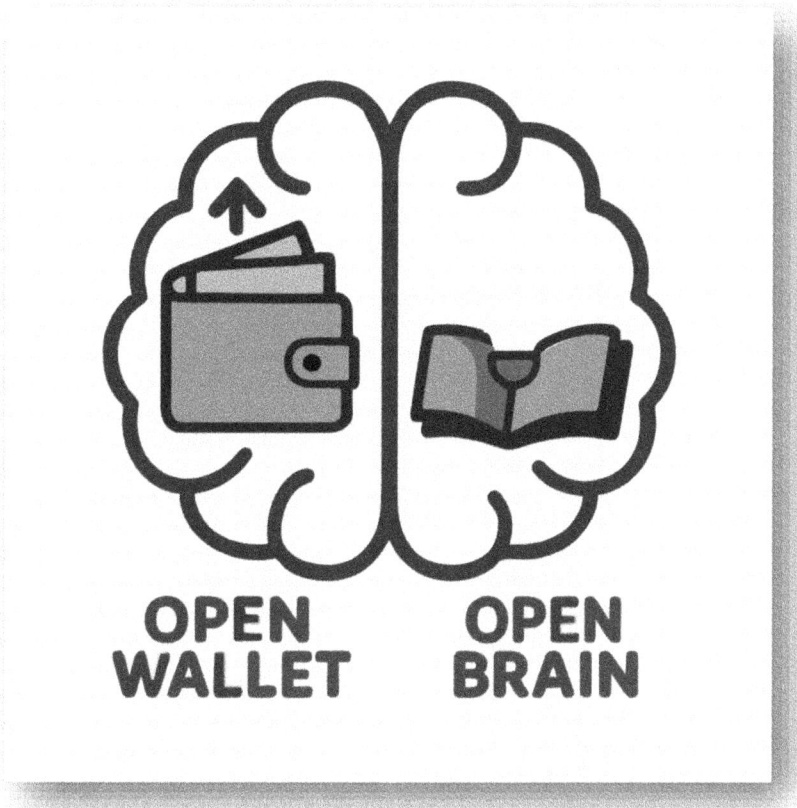

What's Your Money Story?

Most entrepreneurs think their biggest money challenges are external: landing clients, hitting revenue goals, raising capital. But nine times out of ten, the real battleground is internal.

You bring your entire money story into your business-whether you realize it or not.

That story started long before you ever thought about becoming a founder. It was shaped by the household you grew up in, the experiences you had around money as a child, and the cultural narratives you absorbed without question.

Maybe you heard things like:

> *"Money doesn't grow on trees."*
> *"We can't afford that."*
> *"Rich people are selfish."*
> *"Money isn't important; love is."*

Or maybe you grew up in a home where money was taboo - where finances were whispered about behind closed doors, leaving you with a vague sense of anxiety every time the subject came up.

These early scripts sink deep into our subconscious. We rarely question them until they start *hurting* us-showing up as underpricing, hesitating to invest, feeling guilty about making money, or sabotaging financial success just when it arrives.

Here's the catch:

> Your business cannot outperform your personal money mindset.

If you're secretly afraid that making money will make you a bad person, or if you believe there's never enough to go around, it doesn't matter how many marketing tactics you deploy-you'll unconsciously create resistance.

> **Brent's Thoughts™** Here's my money mindset: Thank God I had the parents I had. I was a bootstrapper from an early age. I was saving every penny I could from my allowance to get a comic book, while my brother was probably spending his on candy. Between 12 and 16, I had saved up money from my endless hard work to buy a stereo, a waterbed and a semester in France. So, that's great. Scrimp & save & do it all yourself. That's my mindset. I CANNOT seem to get my head around spending money to make money. It scares the bejesus out of me. My money mindset is part of the reason Drive-By Laundry never did very well and definitely negatively impacted some of my other businesses. The first step is recognizing you have a problem, right?

Founders who don't examine their money beliefs end up:

- Setting prices that barely cover their needs.
- Over-giving to clients out of guilt.
- Avoiding crucial financial planning.
- Burning out because they equate worth with overwork.

Awareness is the first step.

You didn't choose your first money story. But you can choose whether to keep living by it.

Let's start by mapping where you are now.

The Money Mindset Spectrum

Money beliefs aren't binary-you're not either "bad" or "good" with money. Instead, think of your money mindset like a spectrum, a range you move across depending on your experiences, context, and choices.

Here's the **Money Mindset Spectrum**:

The Money Mindset Spectrum

Scarcity → Survival → Security → Sufficiency → Stewardship → Abundance → Overcompensation

Let's unpack these stages:

Scarcity

- Core belief: "There's never enough."

- Behavior: Hoarding, extreme frugality, fear-based decisions.

- Business Impact: Chronic underpricing, refusal to invest in growth, panic at every slow month.

Survival

- Core belief: "I just need to make it to tomorrow."
- Behavior: Short-term hustle, reactive decision-making.
- Business Impact: Chasing low-quality work just to stay afloat, constant exhaustion.

Security

- Core belief: "If I work hard enough, I'll be safe."
- Behavior: Focus on stability over opportunity.
- Business Impact: Building "safe" offers instead of innovative ones, resisting risk even when it's calculated.

Sufficiency

- Core belief: "I have enough, and I can create more."
- Behavior: Balanced earnings, mindful spending.
- Business Impact: Healthy growth mindset, clearer pricing, better investment in self and team.

Stewardship

- Core belief: "Money is a tool to create good for myself and others."
- Behavior: Intentional earning, investing, giving.

- Business Impact: Strategic scaling, philanthropic thinking, energy to serve without martyrdom.

Abundance

- Core belief: "There's more than enough for everyone."
- Behavior: Generosity without guilt, proactive wealth-building.
- Business Impact: Attracting high-value partnerships, clients, and opportunities.

Overcompensation

- Core belief: "I must accumulate to prove my worth."
- Behavior: Workaholism, status chasing, never feeling "done."
- Business Impact: Burnout, toxic growth, damaged relationships.

Exercise:

Reflect for a moment-where do you naturally operate on this spectrum when you think about money and your business? Are you stuck in survival mode, or starting to lean into stewardship? Write it down.

Money mindsets are fluid. You might feel abundant in your personal life, but you operate from scarcity when it comes to investing in your business. The goal isn't perfection. It's awareness.

> Once you see where you are, you can choose how to move.

Common Toxic Scripts (and What They Cost You)

Let's talk about the specific money beliefs that sabotage founders the most. You might recognize some of these sneaky thoughts:

"If I charge too much, no one will buy."

- Root Fear: Rejection, abandonment, feeling "too much."
- Result: Underpricing, resentment, overwork.
- Reality Check: Higher pricing often attracts *better* clients who are more committed.

"I shouldn't do this for the money."

- Root Fear: Guilt, shame, fear of losing meaning.
- Result: Giving away work for free, neglecting sustainability.
- Reality Check: You can serve *and* thrive financially. Profit amplifies your ability to help.

"Once I'm making money, I'll finally feel secure."

- Root Fear: Insecurity, scarcity mindset.
- Result: Constant moving goalposts-never feeling "enough."
- Reality Check: Security comes from your relationship with money, not an external number.

"Good people don't get rich."

- Root Fear: Fear of becoming disconnected, judged, or corrupt.
- Result: Self-sabotage, limiting income potential.
- Reality Check: Money amplifies character. If you're good now, wealth gives you a bigger platform for good.

These scripts aren't just "mindset issues."
They drive real behavior: pricing decisions, investment hesitations, team hires, even how big you allow your vision to get.

If you want to build a business that grows sustainably, you must catch and consciously rewrite these invisible scripts.

Rewiring the Money Mindset

The good news? Money beliefs aren't fixed.
You can rewire them the same way you rewire any other habit: through awareness, practice, and intentional choice.

Here's a process you can start today:

Identify Your Default Belief

Pay attention to the thought that pops up when you think about charging more, investing in coaching, hiring help, or celebrating a win.

Ask: Is This Actually True?

Challenge inherited assumptions.

Example: "People will hate me if I raise my rates." → Is that objectively true? Have I seen examples to the contrary?

Create a New, Empowering Belief

Example:

Old: "No one will pay me that much."

New: "The right people value and invest in what I offer."

Take a Micro-Action to Reinforce It

Tiny steps matter. Raise your rates by 10%. Spend $100 on a growth investment. Celebrate a client win without apologizing.

> **Brent's Thoughts™** Let's talk about the old laundry again. You know, I agonized over price changes in the beginning, and I STILL agonize and procrastinate when I have to send a letter out with price increases (yes! I still run the Drive-By Laundry website - as a favor to the guy who bought my laundromat so many years ago). You know what? I don't think I ever lost a good customer because of price increases.

Use Role Models

- Find examples of founders, entrepreneurs, or even everyday people who relate to money with abundance, stewardship, and responsibility.

- Study how they talk about money and borrow their language until it becomes natural.

All of my financial role models eventually turn out to be monsters. I'm looking for a new one. Who will be my next one? Maybe you!

Remember: you're not aiming to become "perfect" with money overnight. You're building a healthier, more resilient relationship that can sustain the weight of the vision you're growing.

Wrap-Up + What's Next

Money is never just about money.

It's about identity, power, trust, stewardship, and permission.

In this chapter, you started excavating the money stories that have shaped your life-and by extension, your business. You mapped your current place on the Money Mindset Spectrum. You recognized toxic scripts that no longer serve you. And you began the work of conscious rewiring.

The goal isn't to become obsessed with money. It's to become at peace with it; to see it as a tool for impact, not a source of anxiety or shame.

When you heal your relationship with money, you free yourself to lead, to build, and to create at your highest level.

And you're going to need that freedom for what comes next.

Because in Chapter 5, we're going bigger: **Designing Your Life.**
We'll take everything you've uncovered so far: your purpose, your identity, your strengths, and now your healthier money beliefs-and start crafting a vision for a life and business you want to live.

> **Not just success on paper. Success in real life.**

See you there.

Designing Your Life

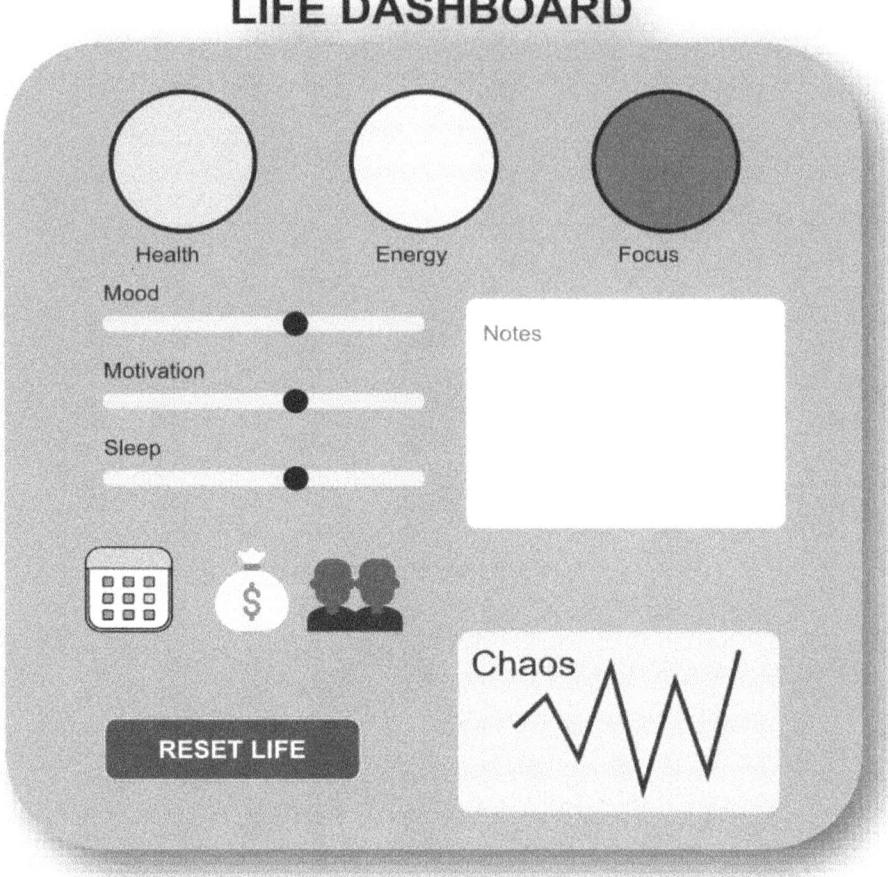

Don't build your business first and wedge your life in later. Design your life first and build your business to support it.

What Does "Life Design" Even Mean?

Let's start with a truth bomb: most founders design a business, not a life.

> **Brent's Thoughts™** Ooh - that smarts! I'm very guilty of wrecking my life building a business. Trying not to do that anymore. Even I'm redeemable though. Remind me to tell you about the time I fired a client that was 1/3 of my revenue, because they decided to take the FAFO path.

They whip up pitch decks, marketing plans, product roadmaps-and somewhere in the scramble, they forget to ask a deeper question: "What kind of life is all this supposed to support?"

Life design is about making that question central, not an afterthought.

If you've ever found yourself building something that technically "works," but leaves you emotionally drained, disconnected from your values, or feeling like your business owns *you*, this chapter is your reset button.

Most burnout isn't from working too hard. It's from working out of alignment.

Instead of reacting to urgent emails and market trends, life design says: Let's get proactive.
Let's build a life you want to live and then reverse-engineer a business that fits into that life - not over it, under it, or swallowing it whole.

Whose Life Are You Living?

Exercise:

Take five minutes and describe a typical week in your life.
Be honest. Write what actually happens, not what you wish happened.

Now ask yourself:

- Where did this structure come from?

- Whose expectations shaped it?

- Is this life energizing you or exhausting you?

No guilt, no judgment-just observation.

> **Brent's Thoughts™** I might be showing a little privilege here, but also I'm very frugal: I live my life in my little neighborhood.. I work most of the day, because I'm excited about what I'm doing. I stop when I don't feel like it anymore. I walk around. I buy bread at my local bakery. I'm actually kind of boring. I wanted this! I made this happen. I don't like driving a lot, so I pretty much walk everywhere. I had to learn to listen.

The Life Alignment Matrix

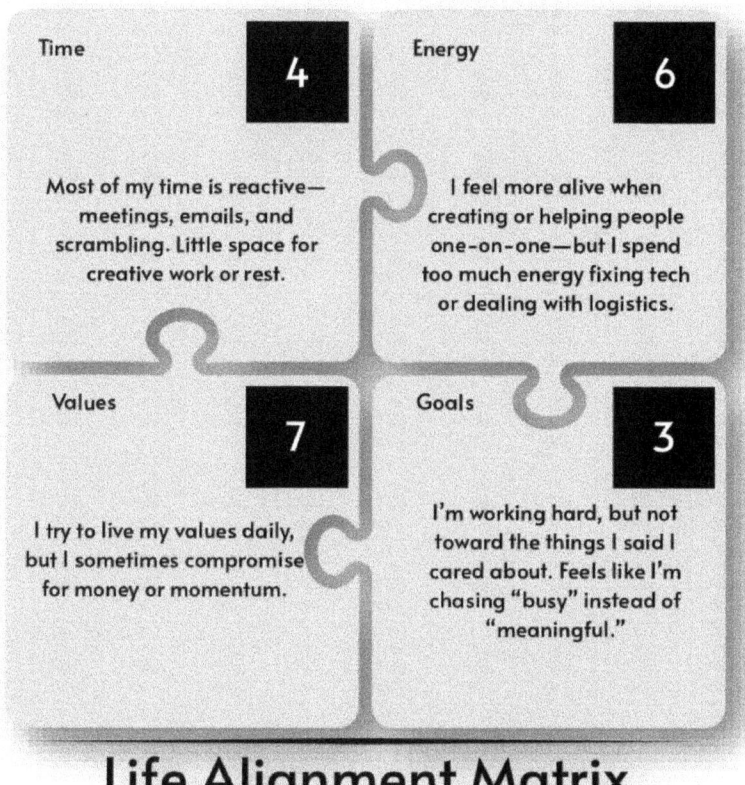

To build a business that serves your life, you first need to know what that life needs.

Enter the **Life Alignment Matrix**, your dashboard for intentional living. It has four quadrants:

- **Time** - How you spend your hours
- **Energy** - What fuels or drains you

- **Values** - What matters most

- **Goals** - What you're working toward

Here it is - a simple 2x2 grid. Each quadrant gets a self-score from 1 to 10 (and maybe some notes):

Time	Energy
Value	Goals

The higher the score, the more aligned that area is with the life you want. Low scores show where friction lives.

Let's walk through each:

Time

- What dominates your calendar right now?
- Do your hours reflect what matters-or what's urgent?

Energy

- What work leaves you energized-even when it's hard?
- What drains you, even when it's "easy"?

Values

- Are you acting in integrity with what you say matters most?
- Do your choices reflect purpose-or performance?

Goals

- Are you pursuing goals that feel meaningful-or inherited?
- Do they serve your version of success-or someone else's?

Add up your scores. Which quadrant needs the most attention? You don't need all 10s. But even moving from a 4 to a 6 can be transformative.

• • •

Reverse-Engineer From the Life You Want

Now that you've measured where you are, let's shift to where you want to be.

Designing your life starts by defining what you want more of, what you want less of, and what "enough" looks like.

Vision Script Workshop: Design Your Future Week

Grab a journal. Take a deep breath.

Now imagine it's three years from today. You've built a business that fully supports your life—financially, emotionally, creatively.

Describe a full week in that life. In vivid detail.

- Where do you live?
- What's the first thing you do when you wake up?
- What kind of work are you doing and when?
- Who are you surrounded by?
- What don't you do anymore?
- How do your weekends feel?

Write freely. Make it feel real, not perfect. Your only job is to capture your truth, not Instagram's.

Examples:

- *A solo founder with a toddler writes: "I work from 9-2 each weekday. No meetings after lunch. Friday is 'no laptop day.' I walk my daughter to school, and we have homemade pizza every Friday night."*

- *A nomadic agency builder envisions: "I work in month-long sprints. I live in a new city every quarter. My team handles 80% of operations. I only take calls on Tuesdays and Thursdays."*

Both are valid. Both are intentional. Neither happened by accident.

When you finish your script, look back and ask:

- What are the non-negotiables?
- What tradeoffs might be required?
- What business models or team structures would support this?

Spoiler: Answering those questions is where we're headed next.

Making Tradeoffs Visible

We live in a culture that says you can have it all. But ask any founder who's been at it a while, and you'll hear a more honest truth:
You can have most things-but probably not everything, and definitely not all at once.

Tradeoffs are real. And wise founders face them head-on.

> **Brent's Thoughts℠** I had to live far from family in a place where the pace was more relaxed and my savings would allow me to have a longer, less stressful on-ramp to success. That's one reason why I lived in Nicaragua and now live in Mexico. I wouldn't change a thing.

Here's what that looks like:

Case Study #1: The Solo Artisan

Sasha is a creative entrepreneur who runs a handmade stationery brand. She loves crafting, hates managing people, and wants full control of her schedule.

She chooses:

- Low overhead
- Limited launches
- Premium pricing
- One assistant 10 hours/week

Sasha caps her income around $150k/year-by choice.

She's optimizing for time freedom and solo joy, not scale.

Case Study #2: The Scalable Strategist

Jordan builds a content agency with a team of contractors and full-time staff. He delegates aggressively and focuses on systems, client acquisition, and high-leverage work.

He chooses:

- Complex ops
- Team meetings
- Quarterly growth targets
- Delegation over perfection

Jordan makes $800k/year-but works 50+ hours, with scheduled vacation blocks.

He's optimizing for impact and long-term equity.

• • •

Neither founder is wrong. But they each made **intentional tradeoffs**.

Life design means owning your priorities-even if someone else wouldn't choose them.

Mini-Exercise: Define Your Tradeoff Philosophy

Answer each pair:

- Freedom vs. Control
- Flexibility vs. Predictability
- Craft vs. Scale
- Simplicity vs. Legacy
- Autonomy vs. Collaboration

Which word pulls you more? What are you most afraid of losing?

Now write a sentence that summarizes your current bias:

"Right now, I'm optimizing for [x], even if it means giving up [y]."

Building a Life-Aware Business Plan

Now that your priorities are clearer, let's plug them into your business vision.

We call this **Life-Aware Planning**.

It flips the traditional approach:

- Old way: "What business will succeed in the market?"
- New way: "What business supports the life I want to live?"

You're not ignoring market needs-you're just filtering them through *you* first.

Business Model Fit Check

Here are four business model components to sanity-check against your life design:

1. **Revenue Model**
   - Retainers vs. one-offs
   - Passive vs. high-touch
   - Hourly vs. outcome-based

2. **Delivery Structure**
   - Live vs. asynchronous
   - Custom vs. productized
   - Solo vs. team-based

3. **Team Needs**
   - Can you stay solo?
   - Do you need systems?
   - Will you hire or partner?

4. **Marketing Strategy**
   - Always-on vs. seasonal bursts
   - Organic vs. paid
   - Personal brand vs. faceless funnel

You don't have to choose "forever" models-but know what matches *now*.

Sidebar: Design Guardrails

Here are a few "guardrails" other founders use to protect their life design:

- "No calls before 11am"

- "No email on weekends"

- "Launch no more than twice a year"

- "Work only when kids are at school"

- "Six weeks on, one week off schedule"

- "Only take clients through referrals"

What boundaries would help your business protect your life-not compete with it?

> **Brent's Thoughts™** I know I sure as hell will never do a business where I have to be on the roads taking things to people at 7am, and I probably won't ever run a business that's location-dependent again. I might be a homebody, but when I need to peace out, I want to take my work with me (sometimes!)

Wrap-Up + Preview of Chapter 6

Let's recap the shift we're making:

Old Way	Life-Aware Way
Build the business first	Design your life first
Fit your life around your work	Build work around your life
Max out potential	Define "enough" and work backward
React to urgency	Prioritize alignment

> Your business is not your life.
> It's the *engine* that funds, enables, and amplifies the life you care about.

So, here's your next question:

Now that you've mapped your ideal life… how do you start living it?

That's where we go next.

Chapter 6 Preview: Habits & Focus

A big vision is nothing without daily traction.

In the next chapter, we'll zoom into the micro level: your habits, rituals, and energy.

- What keystone habits shape your day?

- What's killing your focus (and how do you reclaim it)?

- What does a great *Monday morning* look like in your life-by-design?

We'll help you build the rhythm that sustains your alignment-not just admire it.

Final Reflection Prompts

Before you turn the page, pause and journal on these:

1. What are your top 3 non-negotiables in life right now?
2. What business boundaries would support them?
3. What's one tradeoff you're ready to accept on purpose?
4. What does your ideal Monday morning look like?

Habits & Focus

| You don't rise to the level of your goals- you fall to the level of your systems.

Why Habits Matter More Than Hustle

Let's start with a common founder fantasy:

"Once I get through this launch / project / client sprint / whatever... I'll finally get organized."

We've all told ourselves some version of that. But here's the truth:
If you're always relying on hustle, you'll eventually burn out or break down. What gets you to six figures might be adrenaline. What gets you to sustainability is habit.

That's why this chapter is less about crushing your to-do list and more about designing the engine that keeps you going-without having to white-knuckle it every week.

> **Brent's Thoughts™** I had an ice cream shop once, and I resisted the urge to just operate the whole thing on paper like all my neighbors. It would have been the easiest thing to do in the very short term, but going the extra step to install a point of sale saved me so much frustration and also foiled a couple of attempts at employee theft. I'm definitely guilty of letting terrible systems live for too long. Try not to do that!

Because energy isn't just about motivation. It's about infrastructure.

> "You are what you repeat. And if you repeat chaos, you build burnout."

Whether or not you realize it, your current habits are already shaping your outcomes.

The question is: are they doing it *on purpose?*

Founders often default to what we might call "urgency loops" - waking up reactive, working in stress cycles, finishing the day depleted but unsatisfied. We think we have a productivity problem, when really we have a systems problem.

Habits are the leverage point.

They're small, repeatable patterns that stack into identity.

They create space for focus to thrive-and give your creativity a predictable container to show up in.

And the good news? You don't need a 40-step morning routine with cryo-chambers and turmeric shots. You just need a few well-chosen anchors.

We'll get to those. But, first let's talk about the brain in the founder's head. For many of us, it doesn't operate like a textbook.

Entrepreneurs are overrepresented in the neurodivergent crowd-especially with ADHD. You may not have a formal diagnosis, but if any of this sounds familiar:

- Constant idea generation, but scattered execution
- Hyperfocus one minute, brain fog the next
- "Urgent = interesting, boring = impossible"
- Dopamine as your actual operating system
- Systems that work for 3 days, then implode

…welcome to the club.

> **Brent's Thoughts™** #triggered. Nope, brain definitely not a textbook. Yes, stereotypically ADHD - my leg is moving a mile-a-minute as I type. It's a superpower though. Just needs to be harnessed!

Habits & Focus - 59

ADHD isn't a flaw. It's a founder trait.

You're likely a fast pattern recognizer. You spot connections others don't. You're driven by curiosity, creativity, and momentum.

But your default brain also resists rigid structure. It craves novelty. It wants a reward now, not 30 days from now.

The trick isn't to "fix" your brain-it's to design around it.

> **Brent's Thoughts™** What's working for me right now is to let my unbridled thoughts flow as much as I dare. Scribbling notes in the Strategy Hub as fast as they come to me. But, coupled with that, is a little bit of structure. I identify 3-4 things that are non-negotiable that I have to get done today. This approach works for me. Because I have lots of lists, I can always find something to work on as I procrastinate about doing something else (procrastination is like my dirty little pleasure). So, everything eventually ends up getting done.

How to Build Focus Systems for a Fast Brain

Let's make this practical. Whether you're formally diagnosed or just ADHD-adjacent, these strategies can change your daily rhythm:

Timeboxing + Visual Timers

Break your day into short, clear blocks. Use timers you can see. (The ADHD brain often can't feel time unless it's visible.)

"Work on newsletter for 25 minutes" is better than "Write newsletter."

Body Doubling

Work beside someone (even virtually).

The presence of another person-real or implied-can massively increase task follow-through.

Try a co-working call, or even play a "study with me" video.

> **Brent's Thoughts™** Accountability partners are my zero-to-hero, because I guess I don't care enough to be accountable to myself, but if I have stated an intention to someone else, I owe it to that person to do what I said I would do (even though they probably don't care!).

Dopamine-Safe Rewards

Set micro-rewards for task completion-but make them nourishing. Examples: 10-minute walk, coffee refill, playlist switch, a tiny square of chocolate. Avoid overloading on sugar, scrolling, or shopping dopamine that crashes you (I wish I could say I always heed that advice).

Chunk Your Tasks by Mode

Don't just work by priority. Group tasks by cognitive mode:

- Creative (writing, brainstorming)
- Administrative (inbox, CRM)
- Visual (design, layout)
- Social (calls, interviews)

Switching less = better focus.

Default to Simple, Repeatable Routines

Don't reinvent how to start your day every day. Have a default startup ritual. Even something as simple as:

Make tea → Open To-do list → Pick 1 deep task → 30 min timer

...can train your brain to enter focus mode with less resistance.

> "ADHD isn't the problem. Poor systems are. Great founders don't avoid structure, they customize it."

That's why we don't start with discipline. We start with design.

Up next: let's talk about keystone habits, morning rituals, and what your body might be trying to tell you about your brain's focus fuel.

Keystone Habits & Morning Energy Rituals

Not all habits are created equal.

Some habits create a ripple effect-making other positive behaviors easier or automatic. These are called **keystone habits**, and they're the secret backdoor to transformation.

Examples:

- Regular sleep → better mood, willpower, focus
- Daily journaling → emotional processing, better decisions
- Morning movement → energy, reduced stress, increased idea flow
- Clean desk → mental clarity, fewer distractions

Find the one or two keystones that unlock your best self-and protect them like gold.

> **Brent's Thoughts™** I'm not going to lie and say I practice what I preach all the time, but I do clean my desk whenever I can get myself to do it. It feels almost as good as a haircut. Also, letting out some free-form brainstorms early in the morning keeps my brain rung out and lets me be a lot more at ease all day.

The Power of Morning Rituals

Your morning is the foundation of your focus.

And no, you don't need to wake up at 4:30am, drink buttered coffee, and do 37 push-ups in a cold shower.

But you do need some kind of **intentional launch sequence**.

> The first 30 minutes of your day can either ground you or scatter you.

Here are some founder-tested morning energy rituals you can steal or adapt:

The Five-Minute Reset

- Hydrate
- Open the blinds
- Breathe for 60 seconds
- Choose your ONE priority
- Put your phone in a drawer

The 3-Line Journal

- One sentence of gratitude
- One sentence about how you feel
- One sentence about what matters most today

The Silent Walk

- 10-15 minutes, no podcast, no phone
- Let your brain wander, reset, untangle

The "Deep Start"

- First 90 minutes = deep work, no messages
- No Slack, no inbox, no meetings
- Set a single clear goal and hit go

The ritual itself is less important than its consistency.

The goal is to signal to your brain:

"It's time to be present, focused, and aligned."

Mini-Exercise: Design Your Morning Start Sequence

What's the **minimum viable morning** that gets you centered and intentional?

Write it down. Test it for a week. Refine it.

If you're already using a tool like a habit tracker or planner, make this a checkbox.

Clean Fuel: Diet, Movement & Substances

You can have the best intentions in the world...

...but if your brain is running on sludge, you'll feel it.

This isn't a wellness sermon. It's just founder math:

Clean fuel = better clarity, stamina, mood regulation, and decision-making.

Let's not start beating green leaves to death and making smoothies (unless you're into that), but let's maybe at least trade off the Froot Loops for oatmeal and fresh fruit!

Caffeine, Sugar & the Dopamine Rollercoaster

- A little caffeine = boost.

- Too much = jittery start, afternoon crash.

- Combine it with **hydration, protein, and fat** to stabilize.

Sugar, especially refined carbs, can spike and tank your energy.
Keep it slow and steady when you need long focus blocks.

Alcohol (Even Just a Little)

One drink might take the edge off at night-but the cost is often next-day fog. Sleep quality suffers. Brain recovery lags. Focus gets dull.

> **"That one glass of wine may be costing you a clear morning of creativity."**

If clarity is the goal, experimenting with lower or no alcohol periods is worth exploring-even for a week or two.

> **Brent's Thoughts™** I feel compelled to mention that, 5 months into abstinence from alcohol, I'm down 30 pounds (13 kilos), I'm keeping more promises to myself, I am more productive and creative than I've ever been. It wasn't like I was a problem or blackout drinker, but it was every goddamned day! I'm 54. I thought I was just getting fat and old and mentally slow, and that knee pain was just the new normal. Boy did I drop a decade and a pants size in short order. I can't think of anything beer has done for me, and I don't really miss the ritual of it. So, I guess I'm a teetotaler now forever! I'll tell you a secret: BuildRunKit and this book series one hundred percent would not exist if I hadn't stopped drinking. All this craziness requires all sparks to be firing!

Movement = Mental Maintenance

Exercise doesn't just shape your body. It tunes your **brain chemistry**.

- Endorphins = natural antidepressants
- Movement = better sleep, lower anxiety
- Walking = literal boost in creativity (proven in studies)

Even 10 minutes of stretching or pacing can shift your focus state.

Fasting: The Founder Reset Tool

For some, light intermittent fasting (e.g., 16:8) improves mental clarity and energy.

Used strategically, it can:

- Reduce inflammation
- Improve focus windows

- Increase emotional regulation

Important: this isn't for everyone and shouldn't be used in place of nourishment or medical care. But for founders prone to fog or fatigue, it's a lever worth pulling.

My Anti-Crash Sports Drink + Focus Fast

*This isn't medical advice! Consult your doctor!

Over the years, I've realized I'm either in flow or I'm spiraling. There's rarely an in-between. One of the best things I ever did for my brain and body was creating a simple hydration + fasting routine that keeps me steady during deep work.

Here's my go-to **sports drink** - I felt great all through a 36-hour fast with just this:

DIY Electrolyte Drink (with Potassium Citrate)

- **2 cups water** (or coconut water for extra potassium)
- **1/4 tsp regular salt (sodium chloride)** (for sodium balance)
- **1/4 tsp potassium citrate**
- **1/4 tsp magnesium citrate** (for muscle recovery and relaxation)
- **1-2 tsp lemon or lime juice** (for flavor & vitamin C)
- **1/8 tsp baking soda** (helps with acid balance)
- **Stevia to taste** (optional, for sweetness)

Your body isn't just cargo. It's your clarity vessel.

This isn't about perfection. It's about awareness.

Start asking:

- What foods, drinks, and rhythms give me *clarity*?
- What sabotages my focus (even if it tastes good in the moment)?

Start subtracting what's dulling your edge. You'll feel it faster than you think.

Mind Training: Visualization & Mental Reset

Focus doesn't just live in your schedule.
It lives in your mindset and your nervous system.

Let's be honest: founders juggle stress, uncertainty, and a million mental tabs. Sometimes the thing we need most isn't more willpower... it's a reset.

Mental Hygiene for Founders

Here's a thought: what if you treated your brain like your inbox?
Cleared it out regularly. Filed what mattered. Let go of junk.

That's where tools like **self-hypnosis, visualization,** and **micro-mindfulness** come in. Not as woo, but as maintenance.

> **Brent's Thoughts™** Would you believe - in 2008, when I quit smoking, it was self-hypnosis that finally worked. I mean it really worked. To this day, I revile the smell of cigarette smoke..

2-Minute Mental Practices

You don't need to meditate on a mountain. You just need small rituals that restore your mental operating system.

Try one of these:

Mental Rehearsal

Before a big task, close your eyes and visualize doing it smoothly. Hear the words. See the screen. Feel the result.

This trains your nervous system to approach the task with calm confidence.

Breath Reset (Box Breathing)

Inhale 4 counts → Hold 4 → Exhale 4 → Hold 4 (repeat 3x)

This grounds your attention and resets emotional overdrive.

Scene-Setting Ritual

Pick one playlist or scent that signals "focus mode."
Light a candle. Press play. Open your project.

You're using sensory cues to condition your brain to enter flow faster.

Sidebar: Your Clarity Toolkit

Here's a menu to build your own mini ritual:

- Noise-canceling headphones
- Focus playlist
- Ritual scent or object
- Power pose or movement (before meetings)
- One-word mantra ("Clarity," "Create," "Lead")
- 20-minute timer → reset → repeat

Pick 2-3. Keep them handy. This is your reset protocol.

Build Your Founder Focus Stack

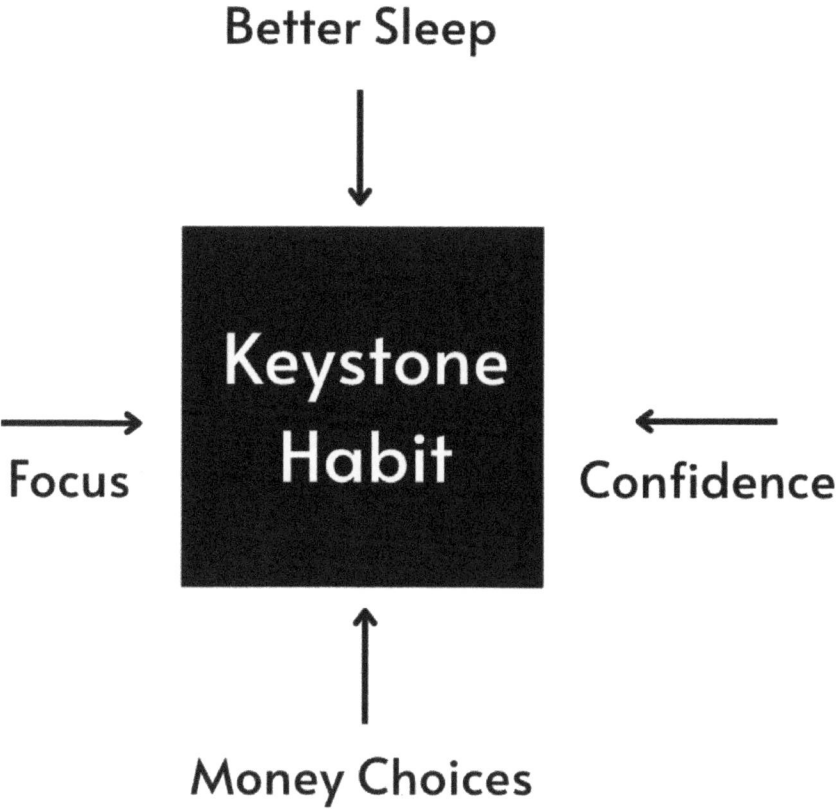

Let's tie it all together.

You've now got a pile of ideas-habits, systems, rituals. But how do you use them?

Answer: you build your **Focus Stack**-a personal operating system for energy and attention.

What's in a Focus Stack?

Think of it like layers that support your best self:

Layer	Purpose	Examples
Morning Setup	Create intentional energy	Journaling, hydration, walk, deep work
Workday Structure	Focus blocks & boundaries	Timeboxing, no-call days, theme blocks
Reset Rituals	Recover clarity after distraction	Breathwork, stretch, walk, playlist
Recovery Habits	Protect long-term performance	Sleep, screen limits, no-alcohol sprints
Safeguards	Minimize sabotage or chaos	App blockers, whiteboards, body doubling

This isn't a one-size-fits-all system.

Your Focus Stack should match your life, your brain, your mission. Mine pretty much consists of coffee and the occasional break to read Reddit posts. Give me a break! I've given up so much already! So much of this comes for free to me now: Less anxiety, better sleep, less doom scrolling, more walking, healthier eating - courtesy of not drinking.

Start small. Pick one ritual in each layer. Test it. Tweak it. Make it yours.

> "The goal isn't discipline. It's rhythm."

Focus Stack Builder

Write yours down:

> ➤ **My best morning begins with...**
> ➤ **My deepest focus happens when I...**
> ➤ **When I lose focus, I reset with...**
> ➤ **At night, I protect clarity by...**
> ➤ **My biggest distraction safeguard is...**

Wrap-Up + Preview of Chapter 7

You now have a system for showing up consistently, not just when you feel like it.

You've learned:

- That habits beat hustle.

- That ADHD isn't a flaw-it's a feature (with the right scaffolding).

- That morning rituals, clean fuel, and clarity tools are the foundation of focused leadership.

- That you don't need 37 hacks. You need *your* 3-5 rituals that work.

This isn't about becoming a robot.

It's about aligning your days with who you're becoming.

> "The founder you want to be already lives inside you. These systems are how you let them out-every day."

Chapter 7 Preview: Support Systems

Now that your internal rhythm is clicking, we zoom out.

In the next chapter, we'll talk about the people, boundaries, and relational dynamics that hold you up when things get heavy.

- Who's in your corner?

- What drains you?

- What does a healthy, founder-friendly support system look like?

Let's build your roots deeper, so your vision can grow taller.

● ● ●

Support Systems

You don't build a business alone, and you don't survive one alone either. Your support system is the emotional scaffolding that keeps you upright when things get heavy.

The Hidden Cost of Going It Alone

Let's talk about founder isolation.

Not the sexy kind, like renting a cabin in the woods to "build in peace." The real kind. The subtle, creeping kind.

- When your partner doesn't get why you're stressed.

- When your family says, "Just get a normal job."

- When your friends nod politely while secretly wondering if you're delusional.

That kind.

> **Brent's Thoughts™** Talk about isolation: I've learned that the quickest way to get into a doom spiral is to promote your book, your project, your product or talk about your successes on social media. God forbid you should ask your friends or family for a book review or a repost. 99% chance you'll get nothing but crickets. No amount of direct messages, tagging in posts will break through with most of your "friends." Don't take it personally. Everybody's got their own lives. They're not your audience. Go ahead and try – you will surely have at least a couple of cheerleaders, but armor-plate yourself mentally, and expect nothing!

Entrepreneurship is already hard. Doing it without a support system? That's like trying to cross a desert with no water and no map, while pretending you're fine.

> *"You may be the one building the thing-but you can't carry it alone."*

The truth is that founders often convince themselves they should do it alone:

- "No one really understands."
- "They'll think I'm weak if I ask for help."
- "It's just easier to handle it myself."

But isolation doesn't make you stronger. It makes you disconnected from perspective, from accountability, from humanity.

And eventually, it costs you:

- Creative energy
- Decision quality
- Emotional regulation
- Even your desire to keep going

This isn't about needing a big cheering squad. It's about being seen and mirrored by people who get it.

It's about letting in support on purpose, instead of hoping it shows up by accident.

Let's talk about who belongs in your orbit-and who doesn't.

Inner Circles vs. Energy Vampires

Not all relationships are created equal.

And not everyone deserves a front-row seat to your business or your life.

This is where founders get hurt.

You share your big ideas with people who don't understand.

You open up to people who respond with judgment, boredom, or backhanded concern.

Or worse: they secretly root for your failure, just so their own risk-averse life choices feel more justified.

> "Your energy is a limited resource. Treat it like oxygen."

Who's in Your Orbit

Here's a quick map to help you clarify:

- ***Supportive & Aligned***

    They cheer for you. They listen without fixing. They reflect your power back to you.
    They don't have to be founders, but they believe in what you're building.

- ***Indifferent or Confused***

    They don't get it and maybe don't try to. That's okay… as long as you stop expecting them to. Not everyone needs to understand. But not everyone needs to be told everything, either.

- ***Draining or Undermining***

    They question your judgment at every turn. They talk more than they listen. They leave you feeling smaller, not bigger. You shrink around them even when you're "winning."

Emotional Access ≠ Emotional Entitlement

One of the most powerful things you can do as a founder is to limit emotional access.

That doesn't mean cutting people off-it means filtering:

- Who gets the early drafts of your ideas?
- Who gets to weigh in on your pivots and pain points?
- Who gets to see your vulnerable moments?

If someone hasn't earned the right to speak into your business or your nervous system, why are you handing them the mic?

Exercise: People & Permission Audit

Draw three circles (like a bullseye):

- **Inner Circle** → Gets full access to your mission, process, and feelings.
- **Trusted Outer Circle** → Gets updates and context-but not raw emotion.
- **Outside the Gate** → Cordial, friendly, but not involved in your founder journey.

Now start populating them. Then ask:

- Who's in the wrong circle right now?
- Who needs to be moved closer in or further out?

- Who are you hoping will support you, even though they've shown they can't?

This is how you stop bleeding energy into the wrong places.

Pattern Break: No More Emotional Self-Sabotage

Here's something nobody tells you when you start a business:

You're going to recreate your childhood dynamics-unless you consciously don't.

> **Brent's Thoughts™** Is there someone in your life you were really hoping to get support & cheer leadership from? Maybe it's a family member or friend that you never asked anything of before. Maybe it's someone who has shown over and over again that your successes just don't matter to them. Don't worry about it, but do make a choice:
>
> 1.) Tell the person your expectations and ask them why they don't support you in the way you had hoped for.
>
> 2.) Erase the expectation from your mind and find someone, who could be a total stranger or someone whom you were never close to, to be that surrogate.
>
> If you've got nobody else, hit the contact form @ https://buildrunkit.com. I still get the messages, and I care!

A little dark? Maybe. But also... kind of freeing.

Because once you see it, you can stop repeating it.

Common Emotional Patterns Founders Recreate:

- **People-pleasing clients**

    You bend over backward to be liked. You undercharge. You overdeliver. You burn out.

- **Parent-boss echoes**

    You hire or partner with people who mirror old authority figures-then feel trapped or small again.

- **Proving energy**

    You build your business not from desire, but from a need to prove your worth to someone who isn't even watching.

- **Bullying dynamics**

    You accept toxic comments from team, clients, or even yourself because somewhere in your history, that felt normal.

    *Pro tip: Call them out! Yes, in public (if that's where they've chosen to FAFO). Make the person feel awkward.

If any of this hits you in the feels, it's not because you're broken. It's because you're human.

But the founder journey brings all of it to the surface. Faster. Louder. And more consequential. I won't even pretend it hasn't all brought me to tears on more than one occasion.

This Is the Chapter Where You Decide:

- I won't hire people who undermine me.

- I won't let old wounds shape new partnerships.

- I won't explain my worth to people committed to misunderstanding me.

You can run a company and still be kind. Still be fair. Still be open-hearted. But you don't have to keep offering up your peace like it's disposable.

> Being emotionally intelligent doesn't mean being emotionally available to everyone.

Building Your Support Circle Map

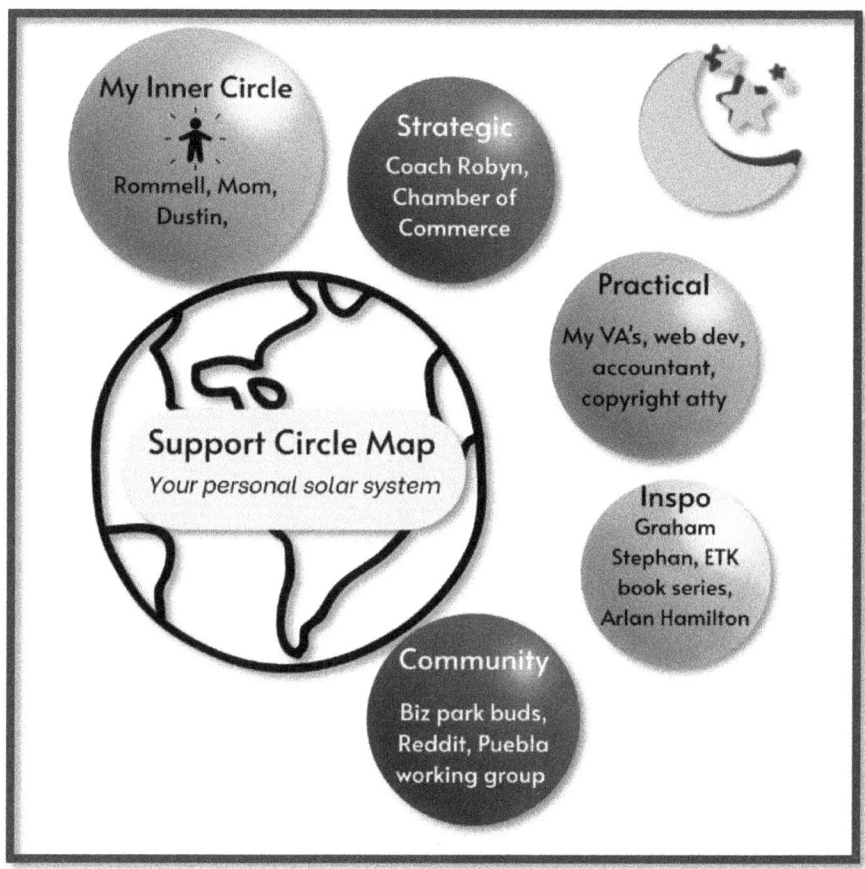

Let's flip the script now.

Instead of focusing on who to remove, let's talk about what to intentionally build.

We're not just talking emotional support here (though that's part of it). We're talking full-spectrum founder scaffolding:

> People who help you think, feel, and move forward.

Your Support Circle Map

Think of this as a strategic design-like a business org chart, but for your emotional and practical sustainability.

Three layers:

Circle	Role	Examples
Inner Circle	Safe, unfiltered, energizing	Best friend, partner (if aligned), trusted coach, therapist, spiritual anchor
Professional Allies	Co-visionaries, sounding boards	Mastermind buddy, mentor, co-founder, lead dev, ops wizard
Extended Circle	Encouraging, casual, shared vibe	Online friends, industry peers, community groups, niche Slack groups

Map It Out

1. Who lifts you up when you feel lost?

2. Who challenges you in healthy ways?

3. Who knows your actual goals (not just the public ones)?

4. Who mirrors back your best self?

5. Who is missing right now?

You don't need a huge list.

Even one person per layer can change everything.

Add Strategically

- A weekly co-working call with a fellow founder who gets you
- A "messy truth" chat thread with your one honest friend
- A monthly walking call with a mentor
- A note page of wins that you share with someone who celebrates, not compares

Don't just wish for support. Design it.

Emotional Labor, Empathy & Founder Sanity

Founders don't just build businesses.

They hold emotional space for customers, team members, collaborators… and themselves.

And that's exhausting.

Especially if you're someone who:

- Feels responsible for other people's comfort
- Can sense when a room "feels off"
- Hates disappointing anyone
- Has trouble separating others' emotions from your own

Yeah. You're a founder, but you also need to be the emotional janitor.

> **Empathy without boundaries becomes self-erasure.**

Signs You're Being the Emotional Hazmat Crew Again:

- You feel resentful even though you agreed to it
- You say "yes" to things just to avoid making someone uncomfortable
- You're managing how others feel about you more than how you feel
- You're over-apologizing, under-expressing, and constantly drained

Sound familiar?

Upgrade Your Founder Communication Toolkit

- Instead of: "Sorry, I'm just swamped right now…"
  Try: "Thanks for your patience. I protect deep work time, so I'm slower to respond."

- Instead of: "Let me know how I can help."
  Try: "Here's what I can offer. Let me know if that works."

- Instead of: "It's fine."
  Try: "That didn't land well for me. Can we recalibrate?"

You're protecting your schedule so you can think clearly, stay steady, and not screw over your future self.

Let's normalize choosing peace over performance.

The Power of Being Seen

Here's the thing: support isn't just about help.

It's about witnessing. It's about being mirrored by someone who sees the version of you you're trying to become and reminds you when you forget.

Sometimes that's a therapist. Sometimes it's a text thread with another founder. Sometimes it's the friend who says, "Hey-I read that post. You *are* making a difference."

Even once a week. Even in passing. It lands.

> **Brent's Thoughts™** You know who sees me? I lived in at Dancing Rabbit Ecovillage for a couple of years (I'm on the board right now!). Seeing people and acknowledging what's important to them is in their DNA. I feel so seen when I'm visiting what, in some ways, I still consider "home." I hope I model that same behavior and that someone will always call me out when I don't.

Reflections That Change Everything

Support is someone who:

- Celebrates your win without inserting themselves
- Asks how you're really doing, then shuts up and listens
- Sees your struggle and doesn't flinch
- Reminds you who you are when you're spiraling

> The antidote to impostor syndrome is trusted feedback from someone who knows the journey.

Make It Real

- Start or join a weekly check-in (3 questions, 20 minutes)
    - What's working?
    - What's challenging?
    - What do you need?
- Create a "mirror folder" in your notes:
    - Screenshots of kind words, client wins, personal breakthroughs
    - Look at it on hard days
- Reach out to someone whose work you admire. Tell them.
    - Founders need to hear it, too.

Support doesn't have to be loud, but it does have to be intentional.

Wrap-Up + Preview of Chapter 8

Let's recap what we've just done:

- You clarified who belongs in your support ecosystem and who doesn't
- You gave yourself permission to stop carrying emotional dead weight
- You recognized toxic relational patterns… and decided to opt out
- You mapped your current support and identified what's missing

- You embraced empathy - with boundaries

You're building something powerful. But you're not a machine.

You need:

- Witnesses
- Anchors
- Protectors of your sanity

Even one aligned relationship can keep you from giving up on your mission.

> **The stronger your roots, the taller your vision can grow.**

Preview: Burnout Prevention

Now that you've built the external support structure, we're zooming back in.

- How do you track your energy over time?
- What are the early warning signs?
- How do you design a business that's not powered by burnout?

Next chapter: we learn to stop running on fumes-and start refueling on purpose.

Burnout Prevention

Burnout isn't failure. It's your system throwing the emergency brake. Your brain, your energy, your relationships. All of them have to stay in balance, or you'll subconsciously burn the whole thing down just to get peace.

Burnout Isn't a Moral Failing

Let's start with this:

Burnout doesn't mean you're weak. It means your system is smart enough to hit the brakes before you drive it off a cliff.

The culture around entrepreneurship tends to glamorize exhaustion - like being perpetually overworked is a badge of honor. But burnout is not ambition gone wrong. It's your body, mind, and spirit saying:

> You're asking me to run without fuel, and I'm not doing it anymore.

What Burnout Really Looks Like

It doesn't always show up in dramatic ways. Sometimes it looks like:

- Staring at your screen but doing nothing
- Hating everything you just created
- Wanting to quit not because it's failing - but because you can't emotionally care anymore
- Building something beautiful and still wishing you could walk away from it

It's not always explosive. Sometimes it's just… emptiness.

You Might Not Even Know You're Burned Out

Especially if you're someone who's used to pushing through.
You think, "I just need a break." But then you take one… and don't want to come back.

Or worse - you do come back, and the joy is gone. The creativity is gone. The you is gone.

That's burnout.

And it's not a sign of personal failure. It's a system failure - a design flaw in how you're running your mission.

> **Brent's Thoughts™** I suffered burnout pretty recently – I was developing a mobile app to support older people and at-risk people who live alone. The thing is, my business partner died, and I just didn't have anyone I could depend on involved in the project anymore. I got it to 90% and just couldn't go on. I learned how to avoid that for future projects, and that's what I'm sharing here. But there were too many bad feelings and I had to just lay the project to rest. Maybe I'll pick it up again someday.

> Burnout is a boundary being drawn by your body, when your brain refuses to.

The Real Cost of Hustle Culture

There's a lie baked deep into startup culture.

It's this:

> ***If you just work hard enough, long enough, and with enough obsession, I'll win.***

That's hustle culture - and on the surface, it looks inspiring. But don't be a boss babe. It's drenched in quotes about grinding while they sleep, outworking the competition, suffering now so you can live later.

But the reality? High blood pressure and exhaustion are not glamorous!

Hustle culture sells you freedom by convincing you to become your own worst boss.

Burnout isn't just from overwork-it's from over-performance.

There's a special flavor of burnout that hits founders:

More than just a mountain of tasks, it's the invisible pressure to look like you're crushing it.

To always be launching, always be building, always be "on." It's performative productivity, and it's a recipe for slow collapse.

You start optimizing everything - until joy becomes a checklist and rest becomes something you have to earn.

You post updates when you're dying inside.

You add features when what you need is a nap.

You smile in Zoom meetings while your stomach churns.

Hustle Works... Until It Doesn't

Let's be honest: hustle works - for a while.

It's a launchpad.

But it's not a sustainable engine.

You can white-knuckle your way through a sprint.

But if your entire business model is "run until something breaks," then the thing that breaks... is usually you.

Energy vs. Output (The Sustainability Curve)

Let's reframe things in founder math:

Strategy	Output	Recovery Cost	Long-Term Outcome
Hustle & grind	High	Huge	Crash & ghost
Balanced rhythm	Consistent	Recoverable	Scalable + stable
Rest-first	Variable	Low stress	Creative breakthroughs

You don't need to stop building. You just need to stop burning to build.

The goal isn't to out-work everyone. The goal is to outlast the version of you who thought that was necessary.

People Who Love You Still Might Not Get It

One of the hardest parts of burnout isn't the fatigue or the fog.

It's the loneliness. When you finally hit a wall and your brain says "no more," your body says, "I'm done," and your spirit just drains, you expect the people close to you to understand.

But often, they don't. Instead, they might say crap like:

"Why are you so stressed? I thought you were doing what you love."

"Just take a break!"

"It's not that bad, is it?"

And suddenly, instead of feeling safe, you feel like a failure with witnesses.

You Can't Perform for Them and Heal Yourself

Sometimes, the people in your life mean well - but they still want you to show up like everything's fine. They want access to the same version of you they're used to.

But when you're burned out, you have nothing left to give them. And trying to fake it? That only makes it worse.

> Burnout recovery requires space. And not everyone will like that.

You Have to Make Them Let You Pull Away

This is where boundaries become non-negotiable.

You don't need to cut people off.
But you may need to stop performing for their comfort.

You might have to say:

- "I love you, but I'm not okay right now - and I need room to come back to myself."
- "I don't need advice. I need time."
- "Please don't take my quiet personally."

Scripts for Sanity-Preserving Boundaries

To a partner:

"I know I've been distant. It's not you. I'm running on empty, and I'm trying to rebuild without collapsing further."

To a friend:

"I'm in recovery mode right now. I still care - I just don't have energy to show up like usual."

To yourself:

"I don't have to keep explaining why I need this space. It's enough that I do."

Burnout Is a Tidal Pull - Let Yourself Go Out to Sea for a Bit

You will come back.

You will feel joy again.

But only if you stop pretending you're not drowning.

You Need Hobbies That Aren't Monetized

If you're like most founders, your first instinct is to turn everything you enjoy into a project.

You can't just garden - you think, "Maybe I should start a vertical farming newsletter."

You don't doodle - you start pricing iPad styluses.

You hear, "you're really good at that," and immediately wonder if there's a Shopify theme for it.

> **Brent's Thoughts™** OMG – I like banana bread and lasagna so much that I started making it for other people during the pandemic. I became like a drug dealer for the homebound.. except it was comfort foods, not crack cocaine (almost the same). Anyway, now my favorite food groups are ruined for me!

Somewhere along the way, we learned to measure everything we do by how much it could earn. In doing that, we forgot how to play.

When Everything Becomes a Business, You Stop Being a Person

Burnout often comes from more than overwork - it comes from identity collapse.

When your only identity is "builder," "founder," "creator," or "hustler"…

…and the thing you're building gets hard, messy, or boring…

…it's not your business that feels shaky. It's you.

That's why you need something that isn't for sale.

Something you do just because it lights you up (in a not-setting-yourself-on-fire sort of way).

The Power of Pointless Joy

Call it a hobby. Call it a creative release. Call it "productive procrastination." I don't care what you call it - just don't optimize it.

It doesn't need to scale.
It doesn't need to grow.
It doesn't need to matter to anyone but you.

Hobby Prompts (That Don't Need ROI)

- What did you used to love as a kid before anyone expected anything of you?
- What would you still do if no one ever paid you or noticed?

- What do you feel a little silly for wanting to try?

Examples from real founders:

- Origami
- Analog photography
- Learning Korean on Duolingo
- Roller skating
- Drawing vegetables wearing sunglasses
- Watching train videos on YouTube

No purpose. Just pleasure.

Mini Exercise: The Micro-Hobby Builder

Create three lists:

1. Stuff I Used to Love
2. Stuff I'm Curious About
3. Stuff That Makes Me Feel Like Myself

Pick one thing from each and try it for 15 minutes this week.
No documenting. No monetizing. No optimizing.

Just let yourself have it.

When you give yourself permission to play, you get yourself back.
And that version of you - the joyful, curious, restored one - is the one who can build sustainably.

The Founder Energy Tracker

Burnout doesn't just show up one day and say "Surprise!"
It builds quietly. Gradually. Systematically.

And most founders don't notice it until they're already toast.

That's why you need a system - not just for time management or productivity, but for energy awareness.

Because your energy is the real asset.
Your calendar doesn't matter if you hate everything on it.

What We Track, We Can Fix

Introducing the **Founder Energy Tracker** - a weekly tool you can use to assess:

- **Mental energy** (focus, clarity, brain fog)

- **Emotional charge** (joy vs. resentment)

- **Physical stamina** (sleep, movement, vitality)

- **Alignment** (how "you" you feel)

You rate each on a scale of 1-10, once a week. It takes 2 minutes.
Then you *listen* to the trend before it becomes a crisis.

Example Tracker:

Category	Mon	Wed	Fri	Notes
Mental Energy	6	4	3	Foggy. Phone distraction ↑
Emotional Charge	5	3	2	Dreaded client meeting
Physical Stamina	7	6	5	Sleep off. Skipped meals
Alignment	8	5	4	Didn't write = lost momentum

After 2 weeks, you'll start spotting patterns.

- Tuesdays always feel better? Double down on deep work.
- Friday alignment dipping? Block it for creative or recharge time.
- Constant resentment? Time for a pricing or boundary reset.

Resentment = Data, Not Drama

That creeping feeling of "ugh, I don't want to do this" is one of your **most reliable signals**. Track it. Trace it. Adjust accordingly.

You don't need to nuke your calendar - just rebalance it toward the stuff that charges you.

Make It Yours

You can do this in:

- A notebook
- A Google Sheet

- A Strategy Hub note board

- Or the printable in the companion toolkit

The tool doesn't matter. The reflection does.

You don't manage burnout with brute force.
You manage it by building a feedback loop between your body, your brain, and your business.

Recovery Systems & The Anti-Burnout Calendar

Most calendars are designed for **output**, not **oxygen.**

They're stuffed with deadlines, deliverables, calls, meetings, and "maybe later" tasks that *never* get deleted.

But here's the problem:

Your calendar is your business model in disguise.
If it's built to bleed you dry, your business is too. It's time to build a rhythm that includes recovery as a strategic priority, not an emergency fix.

> **Brent's Thoughts™** Only sort of relevant – but on calendars that others have access to, I block the shitake out of my calendar availability. If it's an emergency, they'll e-mail you and ask for you to make room.

What Recovery Actually Looks Like

Recovery isn't just doing nothing.
It's doing something that restores you.

We're talking about:

- Walking with no phone

- Laughing with someone who doesn't ask about your launch

- Creating something no one will see

- Cooking a stupidly complicated recipe for no reason

- Sitting on the floor, breathing, and not feeling guilty about it

Build Your Founder Recharge Menu

Create a list with 3 time slots:

Length	Examples
15 min	Stretch, go outside, music reset, nap
1 hour	Long walk, yoga class, drawing, a solo lunch
Half day	No meetings, nature break, full disconnection

Now… schedule them.

Don't wait for burnout to "earn" them.

The Anti-Burnout Calendar

Here are a few rhythms to protect your long-term energy (and sanity):

- **Soft Fridays**

    No client work. No heavy strategy. Just reflection, planning, admin, or nothing.

- **Buffer Weeks**

    After launches or creative sprints, block 2-3 days with zero deadlines.

- **No-Call Zones**

    Choose blocks of time each week when your brain stays undisturbed. Let your calendar breathe.

- **Creative Input Days**

    Consume instead of produce: books, art, music, walks, people-watching, ideation with no pressure.

- **Monthly System Reset**

    One half-day to review your energy tracker, reset your calendar, and ask: what's draining me unnecessarily?

If your calendar doesn't support your nervous system, it's not sustainable - no matter how organized it looks.

> Give your future self what they wish you'd scheduled.

Wrap-Up + Preview of Chapter 9

Burnout isn't weakness.

It's your system **trying to save you** - from a calendar that doesn't care, a task list with no brakes, and expectations you never agreed to.

The longer you ignore it, the louder it gets.
Until one day, you torch the whole thing just to breathe.

But what if you didn't wait until the fire?

- ✓ What if you designed your business to protect the version of you that needs rest, novelty, quiet, and joy?
- ✓ What if your calendar reflected your humanity by design and by default?

✓ What if rest was part of the plan, not what's left when the plan collapses?

You've learned:

- Burnout is emotional as much as it is physical
- People who love you might not understand - and that's okay
- You need hobbies, rituals, and feedback loops for your energy
- You can design recovery into your actual life
- The business doesn't have to break you to succeed

This chapter wasn't about doing less. It was about doing it smarter, softer, and in a way that keeps you whole.

Up Next: Chapter 9 - Personal Runway

Now that you've stabilized your emotional energy, it's time to talk about financial energy.

Because burnout doesn't just come from overwork - it comes from money anxiety, income instability, and pretending you have more time than you do.

In Chapter 9, we'll:

- Build your 6-month financial runway
- Get honest about burn rate, risk, and breathing room
- Protect your mission with math, not just mindset

You don't need to be rich to feel safe - you just need a plan.

Let's make one.

Personal Runway

Your emotional energy keeps you alive. Your financial runway keeps you aloft. Without it, every decision feels desperate - and desperation kills clarity.

Why Founders Need a Personal Runway

There's a quiet kind of desperation that creeps in when you don't have financial breathing room.

> **Brent's Thoughts™** Panic? Me? Never! Oh – except for that one time when my roommate ran up a $900 bill on my phone calling naughty phone numbers. How the hell do you plan for something like that?

You might look calm on the outside, but inside? Every invoice, every slow sales day, every "maybe next month" email feels like someone's stepping on your chest. This is the emotional tax of not having a personal runway.
And it's one of the most common - and most avoidable - stressors in early entrepreneurship.

A runway isn't about luxury. It's about oxygen.

Your runway will be the difference between making decisions from confidence and quiet panic.

Why Most Founders Skip This (and Regret It)

Founders are optimists. We believe things will take off.
We trust the momentum.
We think, "I'll figure it out next month."

> **Brent's Thoughts™** Want the voice of experience? Do you think your super new widget or service is suddenly going to rescue you from financial ruin? Don't bet on it, or at least don't depend on it. I mean, I'm expecting this book series to be a bestseller and in every bookstore and library, but for all I know, you're like the 5th and last person to read it. That's Gloomy ~~Gus~~ Brent's way of telling you to hope for the best and plan for the worst.

And maybe we will.
But that plan only works until:

- A client ghosts

- A launch flops
- You get sick
- Or your brain just… stops cooperating

Suddenly, you're not building a business anymore. You're managing a meltdown.

What a Runway Actually Buys You

- Space to pivot when something's not working
- The power to say no to toxic or misaligned work
- The ability to hire help before you collapse
- Room to test without panic
- The ability to take a week off without spiraling
- It's not about coasting but rather just not imploding the second that life throws a curveball.

> **Brent's Thoughts™** If the success of your project is do-or-die, that's a buzz kill. It's also highly detrimental to your creativity and the quality of your work. You will not be that fun startup founder with the orange socks. Your socks will be gray. Make sure you've REALLY got things covered before you peace out of your 9 to 5!

Mental Framing: "Runway = Resilience"

You can have a brilliant mind and a great business model, but if you're operating one rent payment away from a shutdown?

> It will skew your judgment.
> It will shorten your fuse.
> It will turn you into someone you don't recognize.

> **Brent's Thoughts™** Try taking my Snickers budget away and see if you can recognize me!

This chapter is about changing that.

> You can't focus on your vision if your cortisol is brimming over because of your Visa bill.

The 6-Month Runway Planner

Let's cut through the noise:

Your runway = how long you can keep going without freaking out.

It's not about having fat stacks of cash. It's about having enough clarity and control that you're not making every decision with your back against the wall.

I know I said earlier that you could write to me. Do not write me nor call me because you're out of money. Your Mom called and said not to call her either.

The Formula (Don't Worry, It's Simple)

You only need a few numbers:

- **Monthly Personal Burn:**
  What it costs you to live - basic housing, food, insurance, etc.
  No aspirational expenses. No "just in case I suddenly need a new virtual reality helmet (or underwear)."
  Bare bones, real life, zero flex.

- **Recurring Income:**
  What's coming in reliably (or semi-reliably) every month
  - Retainers
  - Side work
  - Affiliate, royalties, any "low-lift" cash flow

- **Target Runway:**
  You want at least **6 months of core expenses covered** - either through cash on hand, committed income, or a mix.

Example (Let's Do Real Numbers)

- Personal burn = $2,200/month
- Reliable income = $1,200/month
- Runway needed = $2,200 × 6 = **$13,200**
- Gap: $6,000 over 6 months

Now ask:

- Do I have that saved?
- If not, what's my plan to fill the gap?
- Can I reduce my burn without reducing my sanity?

Weekly Runway Review (Seriously - It Helps)

Use the included worksheet or a basic spreadsheet and update it every Sunday:

- Did I spend above/below average this week?
- Any income changes?
- Am I trending toward security or stress?

No shame. No panic. Just data.

You don't have to be rich.
You just have to not be surprised.

Why This Matters Before the Crisis

Most people start planning a runway when they're already nose-down, landing gear half-deployed, engines on fire.

That's too late.

Your runway is what gives you the power to:

- Say no to bad deals
- Give a project room to breathe
- Test something new without betting the house

- Focus your energy without panic in the background

> Hope is not a financial strategy. Clarity is.

The Difference Between Enough and Fancy

Getting a little money is dangerous.

It makes you feel safe - when really, you're just momentarily not panicked.

That's when the fancy creeps in:

- The "deserved" upgrades
- The "I need to look the part" pressure
- The "this sushi dinner is technically a business expense" logic

You start spending like someone who's made it…

…but you haven't pocketed your first million yet.

You've just made it out of the red.

The Trap of "I Deserve This"

Founders fall into this all the time - especially after a win.

You survive a hell month. Land a client. Sell a book.

Your brain goes: I've earned something.

And maybe you have - but the smartest reward is extending your runway, not shrinking it.

Every unnecessary expense shortens the time you have to figure this out.

And the biggest irony?

The less you flex, the more power you keep.

A Personal Sushi Story (1997 Dollars)

I once watched a guy - software startup exec, late 90s - drop **$1,100** at a sushi restaurant to entertain eight people.

This was *1997*.

That's roughly the price of a used car back then.

He was flexing. Impressing. Spending like he'd already IPO'd.

Two years later?

- ➢ That company folded.
- ➢ The checks bounced.
- ➢ The credit cards were wrung dry.

The money wasn't the problem. It was the mindset.

"Enough" Is a Strategic Advantage

"Enough" means:

- You're harder to manipulate
- You can say no more freely
- You don't need to overcharge, overwork, or overperform to survive

You eat sandwiches, not because you're broke, but because you're smart.

You go to the park, not the spa, because your mind needs nature more than luxury.

You don't upgrade your car. You upgrade your focus.

> Fly under the radar. Stack quietly. Move like someone who has options.

Frugality as a Founder's Superpower

You know what real power looks like?

Saying: "No, I don't need to buy that yet."

Not because you're broke, because you're **free**.

> **Brent's Thoughts™** Hey – speaking of freedom: I'm building a technology company right now and writing a 7-book series (among many, many other projects that my chaotic mind has me dancing circles around). I'm hiring employees. Looking for office space. What's my unfair advantage? I'm not living in Silicon Valley. Are you crazy? I'm living in Puebla, Mexico where I can live and perform on a tiny fraction of what I could anywhere in the US (except for maybe rural Kansas or something).

Frugality = Freedom (Not Scarcity)

There's a myth that frugality means living in fear. That it's based in lack. That it's a "poor person's mindset." That's ego talking, and that ego is expensive. Exorbitant. Like, get rid of it!

Real frugality is **precision**:

- Knowing what matters
- Cutting what doesn't
- Letting your values, not your urges, make the calls

Frugal Founders Stay in the Game Longer

While others are:

- Hiring before they're ready
- Buying tech stacks they don't use
- Renting coworking spaces they hate
- Living off vibes and burn rates

You're:

- Keeping your costs low
- Avoiding overhead-induced panic
- Investing only where there's return
- Staying quiet while others burn out loudly

You Don't Owe Anyone a Performance

- You don't need to look successful to be successful
- You don't need an office to justify your ambition
- You don't need to drive anything other than what runs

Let the lifestyle people chase aesthetics.

You're building assets.

Fancy feels good for a weekend.

Frugal feels good for years.

Avoiding Desperation-Driven Decisions

When your bank account is tight, your judgment gets weird.

Suddenly, that awful client doesn't seem that bad.
That sketchy partnership? Maybe not such a red flag.
That "quick cash" service idea you swore you'd never do? Tempting.
Desperation is a distortion field. And once you're inside it, you're not making choices - you're trying to survive.

Money Stress Is a Vision Killer

You started your business to build something meaningful, but when you're scared, meaning gets replaced by metrics. You might stop building and start reacting.

That's when founders:

- Overpromise and underdeliver
- Discount just to close
- Say yes to stuff they hate
- Compromise their boundaries
- Panic-publish, panic-hire, panic-anything

> Desperation erodes discernment.

A Stable Runway = Cleaner Decisions

When your basic needs are covered, even for a few months:

- You're less reactive

- You can filter better
- You start choosing what aligns, not just what pays

That's when real strategy kicks in. When you can pause. Think. Say:

"Is this the direction I actually want to go?"

If You're Already Close to the Edge

That's okay. You're not broken, but now's the time to build a bridge, not make a bet.

Consider:

- Picking up a short-term freelance gig to refill your buffer
- Letting go of something unsustainable to protect your energy
- Being honest about what you can handle

Don't shame yourself for needing money.

Just don't let fear write the next chapter.

> **A clear mind makes better moves.**
> **A funded runway makes a clear mind possible.**

Building Your Realistic Safety Stack

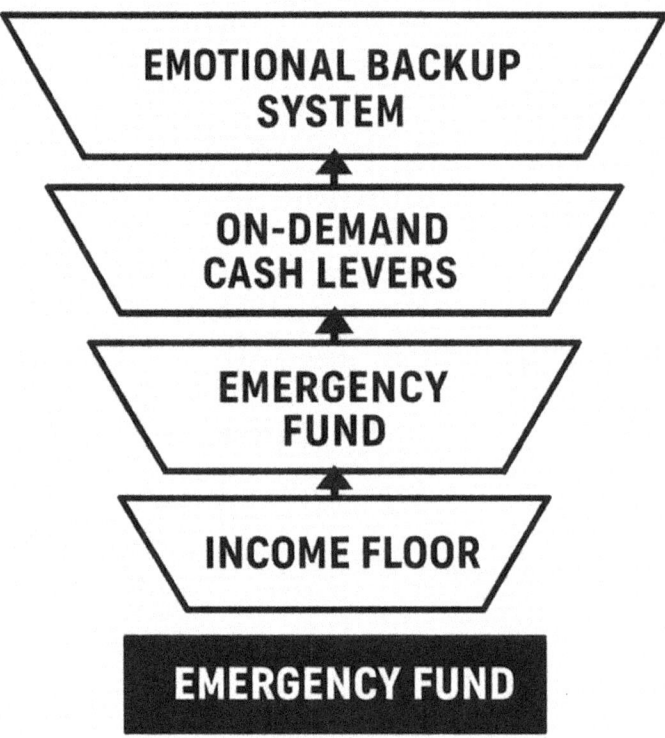

Let's face it: most founders don't need yachts and buyouts. They just want to stop waking up with that tight feeling in their chest every time they check their bank balance.

So, let's stop romanticizing giant exits and start designing something more useful:

A personal safety stack - a set of systems, habits, and backup plans that keep your life from going sideways when business gets weird (and it always does).

What Is a Safety Stack?

It's more than a savings account.

It's a layered system that helps you:

- Avoid panic
- Make smart choices
- Sleep at night
- Buy yourself time to pivot, recharge, or rebuild

Let's break it down.

Layer 1: Emergency Fund

Old-school but still clutch.

- 2-6 months of personal expenses, stashed and protected
- Doesn't have to be in one lump - even $1,000 in a backup account changes your stress levels
- Label it "Do Not Touch Unless the World Is On Fire"

Bonus: Consider a separate business buffer too – at least 1-2 months to cover basics like subscriptions, contractors, etc.

Layer 2: Income Floor

The minimum you can reliably bring in to keep life running.

- Retainers, part-time clients, affiliate trickle, side hustle royalties

- Even a boring hourly gig or 10-hour/week contract can stabilize your brain chemistry

This isn't about ego.
It's about insulation - the space between "I'm good" and "I'm gonna start selling stuff on Craigslist."

Layer 3: On-Demand Cash Levers

"If everything went sideways this week, how could I make $500 in 3 days?"

Create a list. Keep it handy. Some examples:

- Reach out to past clients for quick work

- Package a "bite-sized" offer

- Run a flash promo or beta workshop

- Rent out a skill you don't normally market

- Sell a digital product you've half-finished

You're more resourceful than you remember when you're not in a panic.

Layer 4: Emotional Backup System

Because financial stress bleeds into everything else.

Build a mental toolkit that includes:

- One or two "I get it" humans you can call/text when you're spiraling

- A reminder doc of what you've built so far (yes, really - a brag folder)

- A burn map: What to cut if needed without guilt

This isn't just about money. It's about headspace insurance.

Layer 5: Exit + Recovery Scenarios

Not because you're planning to fail - but because you're smart enough to plan for turbulence.

Ask yourself:

- What's my "I need a break" protocol?
- How would I hand things off or pause gracefully if I hit a wall?
- Do I have a 30-day recovery plan that protects my business and my sanity?

Write it. Print it. Know it exists.

You may never need it.

But if you do? You'll be grateful it's there.

Resilience isn't just emotional strength.

It's knowing exactly what to do when the money gets low and the stress gets loud.

Wrap-Up + Preview of Chapter 10

A strong business isn't built on adrenaline.

It's built on a foundation - and your **personal runway** is one of the most important parts of that foundation.

It doesn't matter how smart your strategy is if you're too stressed to see it clearly.

And it doesn't matter how talented you are if you're saying yes to every bad-fit offer just to keep the lights on.

This chapter was about giving you space - financial, emotional, and mental - to make decisions like the CEO of your life, not from a place of fear.

You've Learned:

- A runway isn't just a number - it's a feeling
- You don't need to be fancy, you need to be free
- Frugality isn't about fear - it's about optionality
- Panic distorts decisions - clarity restores them
- Your safety stack is your true first investor

You're not building a business to impress people. You're building one that lets you stay in the game.

Burnout is emotional bankruptcy. But desperation? That's financial bankruptcy of the soul. Both are preventable, if you design your systems around reality, not fantasy.

Up Next: Chapter 10 - Putting It All Together

In the final chapter, we zoom out.

You've now explored:

- Purpose
- Identity
- Strengths
- Money
- Life design
- Focus
- Support
- Energy
- Runway

In Chapter 10, we'll map how it all fits - visually, practically, and personally.

You'll walk away with a Personal Foundations Map:
A one-page summary of how you, the human behind the hustle, are now supported, aware, and equipped to launch and sustain your next chapter.

Let's finish what we started.

Putting It All Together

You're not a work in progress. You're a work in alignment. This chapter is your clarity checkpoint - a way to reconnect all the parts you've worked through and step forward with a clear, personalized foundation.

You've Done the Work - Now Anchor It

This book wasn't about crushing goals, building a six-figure funnel, or finally sticking to a productivity system.

It was about building something deeper: a foundation.

- ✓ You've reconnected with your purpose.
- ✓ You've reshaped your identity.
- ✓ You've faced the ways money, energy, and pressure have messed with your clarity.
- ✓ You've made space for better habits.
- ✓ You've mapped what support looks like - and what to do when it's missing.
- ✓ You've gotten real about your energy and your finances.

What you've done is kind of like infrastructure.

> **Anyone can launch something. But if your life can't hold it, it won't last.**

This chapter is where we slow down, zoom out, and pull it all together.

You're going to walk out of this with:

- A high-level view of your personal alignment
- A map you can come back to whenever things feel off
- And the next step that's based on you - not what some random productivity bro thinks you should be doing

This is your checkpoint. Your moment of clarity. Your personal launch pad.

Let's build the map.

Introducing the Personal Foundations Map

Personal Foundations Map

Strengths & Habits
Top 3 strengths
_____
_____

Keystone habits you want to protect
_____

Your focus rituals or daily anchors
_____

Support Systems
Inner Circle
_____

Extended Circle
_____

Purpose + Identity
Your North Star
_____

Your current identity shift
_____

Your personal definition of success
_____

Energy Management
Burnout early-warning signs
_____
_____

Recharge rituals
_____

Non-monetized hobbies
_____

Financial Runway
Monthly personal burn
$_____

Runway status
_____

"Enough" number
_____

Safety stack components
_____

This is a tool you'll come back to when things get blurry, stressful, or misaligned. Think of it as your founder clarity compass. A map of you - the values, systems, and support structures that keep your mission grounded and you sane.

The Layout

You can make a simpler version than the one above if that helps. Picture a page split into four main quadrants, plus a center core. It's a mix of identity, capacity, and support.

Center: Purpose + Identity

Why you do this - and who you're doing it as.

- Your *North Star* (one-line purpose statement)
- Your current identity shift (e.g. "From survivalist to strategic," "From freelancer to founder")
- Your personal definition of success

Top Left: Strengths & Habits

What keeps you moving forward

- Top 3 strengths (from your SWOT or real-world wins)
- Keystone habits you want to protect
- Your focus rituals or daily anchors

Top Right: Support Systems

Who holds you up when it's heavy

- Inner Circle (who you trust most)
- Extended Circle (peers, mentors, pros)

- Support boundaries (what you need to ask for / what you won't over-give)

Bottom Left: Energy Management

How you stay resourced

- Burnout early-warning signs (from your tracker)
- Recharge rituals
- Non-monetized hobbies
- Calendar boundaries (e.g. soft Fridays, no-call zones)

Bottom Right: Financial Runway

How you keep breathing room

- Monthly personal burn
- Runway status (in months)
- "Enough" number
- Safety stack components (e.g. cash buffer, backup gigs, emergency protocol)

The goal isn't to fill it perfectly - it's to make the invisible visible.
You're not guessing anymore. You're mapping.

You'll get a worksheet version, but you can also just sketch this out on paper, in the Strategy Hub note board, or even a whiteboard in your workspace.

When things get chaotic, this becomes your re-alignment tool.

It says:

"Here's who I am. Here's what keeps me grounded. Here's how I know when I'm off - and how to come back."

When to Use This Map

The Personal Foundations Map isn't a "nice to have."

It's a navigation system - one you return to when things start feeling heavy, off, or just plain weird.

Because as a founder, drift happens. Not in one dramatic moment - but slowly, subtly, over time.

You get busy.

You stop journaling.

You say yes when you should've said "not yet."

You sign one wrong client.

You skip one week of rest.

Then one day, you wake up wondering why your business feels like it's running you.

Use Your Map When:

- You're stuck in indecision

- You feel misaligned, reactive, or foggy

- You're about to make a big shift - hire, launch, pivot, partner

- You've gone through a personal life change (health, move, loss, relationship)

- You feel burned out, but can't name why

- You just need to remember why you started

Keep It In Sight

This map is meant to be seen, not hidden in a folder.

Post it above your desk.

Print it and pin it in your planner.

Set it as a monthly reminder.

Or make it your desktop background if you want it in your face.

It's meant to be more than a reflection.

It's your reset protocol.

When you feel lost, don't rebuild from scratch. Reconnect with your map.

Common Founder Drift Patterns

No one wakes up and says, "You know what? I think I'll lose myself in my own business today."

But it happens all the time. Not because we're lazy or broken, but because we're builders - and sometimes we get so focused on building forward, we forget to check if we're still facing the right direction.

Drift is Slow - and Dangerous

It doesn't come with flashing lights.

It sneaks in quietly:

- You stop journaling because you're "too busy"
- You take on one off-brand project "just for cash"
- You lose touch with the people who ground you

- You overcommit, again
- You ignore the resentment, again
- You say "yes" when your body is screaming "no"

And before you know it, your calendar looks like someone else's life.

Drift Detection Checklist

Use this anytime something feels off - or as a monthly self-audit:

- Have I said yes to anything I deeply regret in the last 2 weeks?
- Do I feel more dread than joy when I start work?
- Have I done anything creative that wasn't monetized?
- Have I talked to anyone who truly sees me (not just my brand)?
- Have I been sleeping, eating, and moving like someone who respects their body?
- Do I even like the person I'm becoming in this season?

No shame - just data.

> You're not broken. You're just off course. And you already have the map.

What's Next? You're Building Forward

You don't need more planning, just a rhythm.

The point of all this wasn't to become more productive, optimized or intense.

It was to become grounded and intentional.

Progress Looks Quieter Now

You may notice something strange now that you've done this work: Your growth feels… quieter.

Less dopamine, more depth. That's good. That's what real sustainability feels like. The adrenaline high of starting up feels great, but hopefully what will keep you going is knowing you're building something that can last.

Keep Evolving - Gently

You don't need to rebuild this system from scratch every quarter.
You just need to:

- Check your energy
- Update your runway
- Reflect on your support system
- Recommit to your boundaries and your "enough"

That's it. That's the work. You don't need a reinvention. You need a re-alignment. And now? You've got the tools for that.

Wrap-Up + Companion Tools

You made it.

To the end of the book and to the end of a season of guessing, overextending, and wondering if you were just doing this wrong.

You're not. You never were.

You just needed a better setup.

A better foundation.

I hope this helped

- ➢ It was a recalibration.
- ➢ You didn't learn a "framework." You remembered who you are.
- ➢ And now you've got tools to support that version of you - the one who's strategic, sensitive, ambitious and human.

I've done my job if you now feel like someone who:

- ✓ Knows where they're headed
- ✓ Knows what they need
- ✓ Can manage it without burning out

You need to be anchored, and I hope you feel closer to that goal.

Final Note:

This was Book 1 of the Startup Foundations series. For some of you, it might've been the first time anyone encouraged you to give yourself permission to build a business that fits your life. I hope you'll let me contribute to your business's success in a small way by either reading books 2 through 7 or coming over to www.buildrunkit.com and getting the guidance, tools and software you need to launch and run it.

So.. like.. that's it!

JUST KIDDING! Read on for your bonus chapter!

Bonus Chapter: Your Personal Brand

I wasn't planning to include this. Honestly, it probably deserves to be its own book, and maybe someday it will be. But I didn't want to make you buy another one just to get the good stuff. So, here's the express version.

Your personal brand matters — not because you're trying to become some social media personality, but because you're trying to build something as yourself. And if you're going to do that well, it helps to know who you are.

Think of it like this:

If you don't understand what makes you compelling, trustworthy, or different… how is anyone else supposed to?

This chapter will help you:

- Get clear on who you are (in a way that's useful)
- Build your founder elevator pitches (you'll probably have more than one)
- Create a simple, authentic foundation for how you show up online, in person, and inside your business

We're not trying to craft a personal "image" here. We're trying to surface the signal that's already there, so your best-fit customers, partners, and collaborators can meet you where you are.

Let's get into it.

Why Personal Brand Matters — Especially for Founders

Let's get one thing straight:

You already have a personal brand. Whether you've shaped it intentionally or not, people already have a sense of who you are. The only question is whether it's working for you.

> **Brent's Shameless Plugs™** I wanted to highlight that there's an opportunity here. You can visit https://www.buildrunkit.com. We have a tool for this. We can help you discover and document your personal brand(s) and even write your elevator pitches for you. None of it is rocket science though, so carry on..

For founders, especially in the early days, your personal brand does a lot of heavy lifting:

- It builds trust before your product is fully formed.
- It gives people a reason to take a bet on you.
- It helps attract early customers, supporters, and collaborators.
- It sets the tone for your whole business; not just the vibe, but the values and voice too.

People don't buy ideas. People buy from people. Most of the time, they're buying more than your product. They're buying you and your conviction and your story. Your "I'll figure it out" energy.

Especially if you're building something scrappy, new, or a little weird (which, let's be honest, you probably are), your personal brand can be the anchor that holds everything together and the magnet that pulls people in.

If you're raising money someday, your brand will help investors believe in the vision (and in your ability to execute it). If you're trying to hire someone better than you, your brand makes them want to come along for the ride. And if you're selling… well, you're selling yourself long before anyone reads your features list.

So no, this isn't optional. It's foundational.

You don't need to fake anything. But you do need to understand, own, and express who you are — so the right people can find you and say, "I want what they're building."

What a Personal Brand Is (and Isn't)

Let's clear something up right away:

A personal brand is not your logo, color palette, or the fact that you use the rocket emoji in your Twitter bio.

Those things might support your brand, but they're not the brand itself. Your personal brand is the clear, consistent expression of who you are, what you stand for, and how you show up.

It's:

- Your voice and how you talk
- Your beliefs and what you care about
- The energy you bring to a room (or a call, or an email)
- The story people tell about you when you're not around

It's not:

- A polished LinkedIn post that sounds nothing like you
- A fake "authentic" persona
- Trying to be all things to all people

When done right, your personal brand acts like a filter.

The right people resonate with it. The wrong ones opt out. That's a good thing.

A Few Example Brand Snapshots

Here are three rough "brand blurbs" (you'll write your own soon), followed by what their elevator pitches might sound like:

The Thoughtful Systems-Builder

"I'm the quiet one in the room — but I've already mentally rebuilt your process before you finish explaining it. I care about clarity, logic, and building things that actually work."

Elevator Pitch:

"I help overwhelmed founders turn their chaotic workflows into clean, scalable systems. I'm the kind of person who color-codes their Google Drive and knows how to automate your Tuesday morning."

The Magnetic Firestarter

"I show up with big energy and bold ideas. I'm the spark that gets people excited — and the person who stays to make sure it actually happens."

Elevator Pitch:

"I help early-stage startups find their voice, rally their tribe, and launch like they mean it. I'm part hype man, part execution engine."

The Empathetic Guide

"I've been through it. I know how hard it is to start over, or start from scratch. I build trust quickly, and I'm not afraid to sit in the hard stuff."

Elevator Pitch:

"I work with solopreneurs who feel stuck. Together we untangle their goals, rebuild their confidence, and create a path that truly feels right, not just productive."

Each of those founders could be selling the same thing: coaching, consulting, software, whatever. But their personal brand is the difference in how they attract people, how they pitch, and what kind of business they ultimately build.

So... what's yours?

Coming Up:

In the next section, we'll walk through how to build your brand snapshot and craft a few founder elevator pitches of your own - simply a version of you that makes sense to others because it makes sense to you.

How You'll Use Your Brand Over Time

Your personal brand isn't a one-time asset. It's a long-term lever — one that grows in value as your experience, reputation, and network grow with it.

It starts small. Maybe it's just how you introduce yourself in a DM or how your email sign-off sounds. But eventually, your brand becomes:

- The reason someone reaches out with an opportunity
- The "why" behind a customer referral
- The way your audience grows — even while you're sleeping

Let's break it down by stage:

Early Stage (Right Now)

At the beginning, your personal brand fills in the blanks your business can't yet. You don't have traction? Cool. You have a story. You don't have fancy design? No problem! You have a voice that feels real.

Right now, your brand shows up in:

- Your LinkedIn bio
- Your email signature
- Your "about" page
- Your intro messages, outreach, and sales calls
- Your first impressions (in real life and online)

You're building familiarity and trust before the business is even fully built.

Mid-Stage (Growing)

Once you've got some momentum, your brand starts to do more heavy lifting. It becomes a trust multiplier, especially if you're:

- Pitching investors
- Trying to hire people better than you
- Getting featured in podcasts or newsletters
- Starting to get inbound leads

At this point, people are buying you just as much as they're buying what you sell.

Long-Term (Evolving)

Your personal brand doesn't retire — it evolves.

Eventually, your brand becomes an asset that:

- Launches your next product or company
- Sells your book or course
- Gets you invited to speak, teach, consult
- Attracts press, partners, or co-founders

And unlike most assets, this one travels with you wherever you go. You're building more than a company. You're building your personal reputation. One that compounds over time, if you shape it intentionally.

Next up: we'll build yours. Keep it short, honest, and useful — so it grows with you, not against you.

Crafting Yours: A Guided Exercise

This doesn't need to be perfect. In fact, if it sounds too polished, you're probably doing it wrong. The goal here is clarity, not performance.

We're going to build your Brand Snapshot — a short, honest summary of who you are, what you bring to the table, and how that shows up in your business. Then we'll translate that into one (or more) versions of your Founder Elevator Pitch.

Step 1: Start With Raw Material

Grab a notebook, doc, or use the space below if this is printable. I'll leave a little space in case you're a messy Marvin like me, who writes in his books.

Jot down a few answers to these prompts:

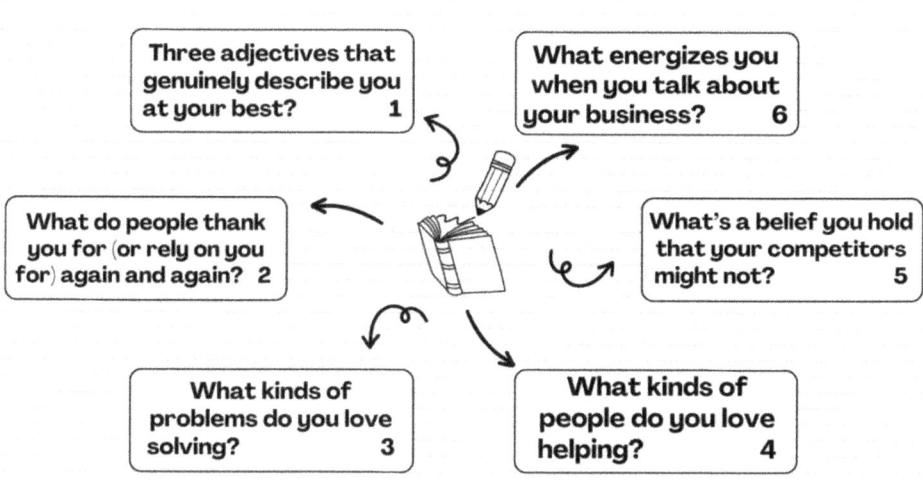

Don't overthink it. We'll clean it up in a minute (umm.. if you wrote in pencil).

Step 2: Spot the Patterns

Look at what you wrote. You'll probably see a few things repeating — certain qualities, values, or phrases that feel true. Pull those into a short paragraph (2–4 lines) that reads like a little intro or vibe check.

Call this your Brand Snapshot.

You're not trying to be universal. You're trying to be you, consistently.

Example:

"I'm calm in chaos and good with people who don't know where to start. I like helping others get clarity and feel confident moving forward. My work is simple, human, and practical."

Step 3: Craft Your Elevator Pitch (or Pitches)

Now, translate your snapshot into something you could say out loud when someone asks,

"So what do you do?"

Try using this format (but feel free to change it up):

"I help [who you help] do [what you help them accomplish], so they can [outcome or result]."

Then, add a human layer:

"Basically, I'm the kind of person who [adds a unique quality or anecdote]."

You might write a few versions — one for clients, one for collaborators, one for the podcast you'll eventually be on.

Step 4: Pressure Test It

Once you've got a version you like:

- Say it out loud.

- Try it in a DM or bio.

- See how people respond.

If it feels like it fits you and makes other people go "Oh, that's cool," you're on the right track.

If it feels like a job interview answer or something you copied from someone else's bio, go back and rough it up a little.

Up next: how to use this in real life without sounding like you're trying too hard.

> **Brent's Thoughts™** Let me help you here – just stand in front of the stupid mirror for 20 minutes, trying on your pitch as if it were a fancy outfit. Keep saying it until you believe it! Check your facial expressions (natural and positive). Remember when you went to the first place you had to wear a suit? How awkward was it at first? After a while, you settled into your new suit, and it probably felt comfortable (except for the fact that suits are usually created by sadistic people that thrive on people being uncomfortable). So, yeah – this is like that.

Putting It to Work

Now that you've got your brand snapshot and elevator pitch, let's talk about how to use it without sounding like a try-hard or giving LinkedIn influencer energy.

You don't need to print it on a mug. You just need to let it shape how you show up.

Where It Shows Up (Without You Even Trying)

Your personal brand seeps into:

- Your About page

- Your social bios
- Your intro emails and DMs
- How you describe what you do at parties (and on calls, and in the pitch room)
- The way you onboard clients
- The content you post (or don't)
- The partnerships you say yes to (and the ones you avoid)

Think of it like scent. You don't need to wave it in people's faces, but it should linger after you leave the room.

Let It Be a Filter

You're not building a brand to please everyone. You're building a brand to attract the right people and repel the wrong ones. That's not a bug. That's the whole point.

When you show up consistently, you'll start to hear things like:

- "You're exactly what we were looking for."
- "I feel like I already knew you before this call."
- "You said something in your bio that really stuck with me."

That's when you know it's working.

And It Evolves With You

You're not carving this in stone. Your voice, focus, and positioning will shift as your business grows. That's normal. Your brand is alive — just like you are.

The more you show up as yourself, the more magnetic, resilient, and scalable your business becomes.

So, take the pitch you've built, the brand you're starting to define, and go wear it out into the world a little. Practice until it feels like it fits. Tweak it when it doesn't. Keep the parts that feel true.

This isn't fake-it-til-you-make-it.

This is say it until you believe it — because it was always true to begin with.

• • •

So now that's it — don't ask me for any more bonuses or chapters. I won't do it!

...Until the next book in the series, which is:

Only Your Mom Cares About Your Idea

A Startup Validation Guide

Because let's be honest: most startup ideas die not from bad code or lack of hustle, but because nobody really wanted them in the first place. In this next book, we'll get brutally honest (and incredibly practical) about testing whether your idea is worth building… or whether it's just something your mom thinks is cute.

It's time to find out if your idea has legs — or just a warm hug and a participation trophy.

See you there.

Your Companion Tools (Available at https://brkit.vip/books - use the password gimmeit)

- **Purpose Pyramid Worksheet**
- **Founder Identity Prompts**
- **SWOT + Strengths Builder**
- **Money Beliefs Reframe Tool**
- **Keystone Habit Tracker**
- **Support Circle Map**
- **Founder Energy Tracker**
- **6-Month Runway Planner**
- **Personal Foundations Map**
- **Reflection Journal Companion** (for all 10 chapters)

These aren't homework.
Hopefully, the tools help you apply your knowledge.
Pull them out when the noise gets loud again.

If You're Ready for What's Next...

- Join the community at brkit.vip/books

- Start using the BuildRunKit to plan your next business, using the Startup Launch Journey guided toolkit. Visit www.buildrunkit.com

- Explore Book 2: **Only Your Mom Cares About Your Idea – A Startup Validation Guide** , where we help you get honest about your idea, put it through the wringer and see if it has legs.

If I can do anything or answer any questions – just drop me a line. brent@buildrunkit.com

Index

6
6-Month Runway Planner, 107

A
ADHD, 59, 60, 62, 72
Alcohol, 65

B
Basecamp, 4
Beliefs About Money, 32
Boundaries, 20, 94
BuildRunKit, 10
Burnout Prevention, 89
Business Model Fit Check, 53

C
Case Study, 50
Common Emotional Patterns, 80

D
Designing Your Life, 43
Diet, 65
Drive-By Laundry, 2, 24, 34, 41

E
Elevator Pitch, 143

Embodying the Founder Role, 20
Emotional Hazmat Crew, 85
Employee Mindset, 19
Employee to Entrepreneur, 18
Energy Vampires, 76
Energy vs. Output, 92
Entrepreneur Mindset, 19
Entrepreneurial Identity, 17

F
Fasting, 66
Focus Stack, 71
Founder Energy Tracker, 98
Founder Mini-Assessment, 28
Frugal, 114

H
Habits & Focus, 57
Hobbies, 95
Hustle Culture, 91

I
Identity Shift Diagram, 16
imposter syndrome, 15, 28
Inner Circles, 76

K

Keystone Habits, 62

L

Life-Aware Business Plan, 52

M

Mental Hygiene, 68
Microsoft, 2, 15

P

Patagonia, 4
Personal Brand, 133
Personal Foundations Map, 125
Personal Runway, 104
Purpose, 1

R

Role Models, 41

S

Safety Stack, 117
Sara Blakely, 4
Spanx, 4
Sports Drink, 67
Strengths, Skills & Blind Spots, 23
Support Circle Map, 82
Support Systems, 74
Sushi Warning, 112
SWOT Analysis, 25

T

The Life Alignment Matrix, 46
The Money Mindset Spectrum, 35
The Purpose Pyramid, 6

Bonus Chapter: Your Personal Brand

www.ingramcontent.com/pod-product-compliance
Lightning Source LLC
LaVergne TN
LVHW061615070526
838199LV00078B/7291